My Husband Died,
Now What?

*A Widow's Guide
to Grief Recovery
&
Smart Financial Decisions*

Debra L. Morrison, CFP®, MS, AEP
Certified *From Heartbreak to Happiness*® Grief Coach

Heartiest thanks to my esteemed
editor, Dr. Virginia R. Mollenkott,
whose patience is unparalleled.

Book Jacket: Rose Spisak
Book Title: Bryce Winter & Juliet Johnson

ISBN 978-0-9904154-0-4

Dedication

*To all women whose hearts have been
broken…healing lies ahead.*

ℭℬ

*I'll bet you've had about enough of people telling
you how strong you are and how great you're
doing during this awful difficult period in your
life…. All I care about is that you ask for
what you need, lean on those who love you, and
try to trust me when I say that you'll come out
the other side.*

Jeannie Hund,
Personal Expressions
Greeting Card

Foreword

Debra Morrison's book provides life-coaching for those widows in need of encouragement and guidance. It teaches survivor behavior. Fear can protect us from real threats, but when one lives in fear, it can be self-destructive.

I have long advocated "don't fear change, change fear." Morrison, too, gives simple-to-follow strategies to change fear. She provides information and insights so that fear will no longer be an issue.

You will learn to listen to your own speech and writings, boldly acting on your own truth when emotional and financial decisions must be made. Combining Morrison's guidance and your own inspiration will create the future you desire.

Bernie Siegel, MD author of *The Art of Healing* and *365 Prescriptions for the Soul. www.berniesiegelmd.com*

Preface

You have a support team, and I'm on it. I use my 36+ years' wisdom as a CERTIFIED FINANCIAL PLANNER™ and Accredited Estate Planner, to filter the risks you need to pay attention to, and coach you on what you can (and should) ignore, saving you considerable time and frustration.

With my Master's Degree in Retirement Planning, I manage many clients' investment portfolios. Yet the specific times in my financial planning career when I felt I'd really made a difference were when I was simply "human"-- caring and empathetic with my clients, particularly widows. Ultimately, it's all about our relationships.

I've helped clients through their own life-shortening diagnosis, burying their spouses and their children, and losing jobs, all the while wishing I had a psychology degree in addition to my financial credentials. Countless experiences have shown me I have common sense and a huge heart, and while those two attributes had served me and my clients well, I didn't feel it was enough.

So I enrolled and trained for two years at the Grief Coach Academy--which sadly is on an extended hiatus--learning specific techniques and strategies to help people process their grief so they could move on to their next chapters with confidence. We coached and were coached for hundreds of hours using several different proven strategies, witnessing breakthrough after breakthrough. I was humbled and proud to be recognized as the Academy's 2012 Grief Coach of the Year.

My hope is to save you grief, time and money with my advice and tips. In that spirit, I have shared a boatload of information for you to be able to reference as you need. If you choose to read straight through the book I'll advise that you skim certain sections the first time through, for a deeper dive into certain chapters later; akin to surveying the ocean before you enter in to swim.

Please be at least as patient with yourself, then, as you would be with your kids or nieces when they're learning. We don't expect them to exit the vaginal canal as Rhodes Scholars, so let's not hold ourselves to a different standard.

Through no fault of your own, you have been thrust into what may be referred to as "foreign territory" without a map, and/or notice. Because I feel strongly that understanding financial jargon is important, I've defined some useful financial terms (in English, not financese) at the back of the book.

This Two-Part book serves as your navigation guide--complete with a combination of valuable information, strategies, hints and hope--to support you both in the early and advanced stages of grief. We'll interweave emotional recovery tools with smart financial strategies, again using plain English, in a fashion that is easy to understand and implement. I sprinkle helpful websites throughout and then list them alphabetically by topic at the end of the book for your ready reference.

Part I speaks to the new widow's emotional well-being and also gives easy-to-follow tips for getting organized. I give you a short list of people and agencies to contact as well as instructions on what information to glean from various financial sources.

Because you've suffered a horrific shock to your body and psyche, I advocate a No-Decision Zone for the first six months. I encourage you first to take small steps towards rebuilding your health and collecting information about your wealth.

You'll:

1. Discover where you are emotionally and financially.
2. Locate your investments, assets, and insurances and organize them in an easy-to-understand exercise.
3. Identify the questions that will need answered in the next six months to 1 year.
4. Refrain from making any large financial decisions until a few months pass.
5. Surround yourself with appropriate professionals and friends who will be available when you need them.

Part II is chock-full of confidence builders, strategies to begin the re-creation process for your life, and money-saving strategies as you face the ever-important Decision Zone.

I have met far too many widows who have survived the darkest hours of grief and yet weeks, months or years later they still feel "adrift in the sea of uncertainty." They're facing overwhelming despair about the unknown without their husband and have no idea what to *do* next.

They **fear doing the wrong thing(s)** for themselves and those who love them; **so** paralyzed by pain and loss, **they do nothing.** By not taking action, they miss valuable opportunities to create meaning in the life they still have to live.

That said, **I have also met far too many widows swindled by financial "advisors" who swoop in with unparalleled speed to "help."** Sadly, some financial salespeople make used car salesmen look like choir boys by comparison. It is very easy to be sold financial products that really, really do NOT serve your best interests, but rather benefit the salesperson with a big, fat commission. The penalties to extricate yourself from such products are prohibitive!

I recommend that your first step will be to retain a fee-only Certified Financial Planner™ who does not sell any financial product, nor earn any commissions whatsoever. Rather, they are paid a fee for their advice on investments, legal, tax, budgeting, cash flow, college savings and risk management—the whole financial waterfront. They will stand with you as your ally and trusted advisor throughout each phase of your recovery, offering recommendations that are tailored to your needs and your needs only, as described in Chapter 12.

If for no other service than to carefully analyze all your Social Security benefit options and advise you best which benefits to take at what age, hire a fee-only CFP®. This is the single biggest decision for many widows and I've seen mistakes cost widows several hundred thousand dollars! Avoid making hasty decisions.

Finally, I am keenly aware that processing grief renders us tremendously vulnerable and that widows' emotions run high. So, while I mean no ill will, I can almost guarantee that something in this book will strike someone as insulting, condescending, or perhaps even rude.

Simply pass over anything that is upsetting for now, please, and read on to a section that feels empowering.

FREE BONUS: Here's my video interview with Jean Burgdorff; one widow's story of how she moved through grief. Hopefully it can serve as a beacon of hope for you, too. Watch it here: www.DebraLMorrison.com/Interviews

Table of Contents

Part I

Chapter 1
Picking Up Your Emotional Pieces

Widowed: even the word sounds hollow. Who wants to self-identify as "widow?" Shocked, terrified, saddened, angry, remorseful, bitter, paralyzed and numb are fitting adjectives. You may have cried out or screamed "Why?" or "Why me?!" or "Why now?!" And you may fear "What next?" as if you may need to gird up yourself now, in case your wounds may be peeled open again and perhaps salt poured in. "Could I BE in more pain?"

The past is the filter by which we see things now. I invite each of you to notice and gain an awareness of who you are and where you are *right now*, as a way of quelling some of the obsessing either about where you were, or where you *should* be.

Granted, what once brought you peace may now instead cut through you like a hot knife; what you once thought you controlled is now whirling, seemingly out of your control. What skills you once possessed and took for granted have now gone into temporary hiding. What you once feared is now laughable. The abject fear of death no longer grips you; it's happened, you are forever changed, and now you live differently.

You've been stopped short. You may have had a warning, perhaps not. Regardless, you've survived one of the biggest "pattern interrupts" of your lifetime. You can expect and believe it is totally natural for you to be confused and disorganized, if not downright scatter-brained.

And I want to move us from "What next?" to the different question, **"What's** next?" Simply by adding an "s" we've shifted our focus from helplessness to strategizing our future, however uncertain.

I don't begrudge anyone who is grieving the death of their husband; the loss is horrendous and unspeakably painful. Precisely because of that, I want to usher in glimpses and then windows of hope for a survivor as quickly as plausible, utilizing my grief coach skills.

I do believe everyone is doing the best they can with the resources they have at any one particular time. And yet I also know that there are more and more resources that could help widows take a chance on discovering or creating a more peaceful today and tomorrow. No, you will never forget your husband; that's certainly not the objective. Yet since you can't change the past, nor has any widow ever changed the past, the new task is to seek any way possible to move through your dazed paralysis with successive baby steps.

The new task is to focus on who you can be, rather than who you were. Your husband would want you to focus on just that.

Through your profound sadness and buckets of tears, you can eventually *re-member* (what otherwise may have felt *dis-membered* earlier in the space of a mere split-second) or *re-join* your internal operating strategies, your inner strengths, and your faith in yourself or perhaps One larger than you.

"How can I possibly concentrate with all these emotions rushing through my heart and my mind?" you may ask. People do. Women and widows do. And as you are able, you will do so too, step by step, idea by idea, feeling by feeling, asking for and learning to receive help from those best able to provide it.

However well-meaning your friends and family may be, if they're not widowed, it is best that you seek out and connect with other widows for support. Women who have ridden similar emotional roller coasters and have been ostracized by certain of their friends have a first–hand appreciation of your need to hole-up and then go, go, go. They, too, have cried a river or screamed till they were hoarse. You can often exchange a world of knowing through a mere glance or hug or embrace. Do connect.

Summary Takeaway:

Feel. It's natural AND healthy. Remember and honor your inner strength; it will carry you through. Seek out and connect with other widows for support and signs of hope.

Chapter 2
Grief Is Sad and Normal

Most likely you have already contacted your Pastor/Priest/Rabbi/faith community and the Funeral Director, so that the funeral arrangements and/or memorial services for your beloved have been handled and finished. If not, the book entitled *Readings for Remembrance* by Eleanor Munro offers myriad sample readings that you may wish to include in your husband's memorial service.

Once the formal proceedings are over, your new life begins, often in stark measure. The family has left, too many friends become mute, and the train of frozen casseroles has screeched to a halt.

It's important to understand that you are not alone in wondering how to deal with death. Despite the 2014 US Census Bureau reporting that some 13 million widows live in the US alone--and of that 4 million are under age 65-- American society **still** doesn't know how to deal with death.

In the mid-1960s, Dr. Elizabeth Kubler-Ross began her landmark research on death and dying, by asking her fellow doctors if she could speak with their dying patients. None cooperated because they were unwilling to admit that they indeed, had any patients who were dying.

Sadly, American society has not made sufficient progress over these last 50 years to truly help people grieving the loss of loved ones, including, specifically, widowed women.

Be prepared for your friends and even family to somehow *forget* your husband's name. They somehow think that saying his name might remind you he's gone. Like you forgot?

Your uttering your husband's name will not only give you comfort, it will also serve as the "okay" others may need to do likewise. Hearing your husband's name uttered is music to your ears. Say it, say it often. Say it in private, say it in public. A recent acquaintance, Fran said to me, "my friends thought that saying my husband's name would make me cry. Not mentioning his name breaks my heart."

Realizing that the shock of death tends to render our brains less effective in the near term, forgiveness for mental lapses is very necessary indeed. Walking into a room and standing there wondering why you walked into that room is a typical example of how one's mind may become compromised due to the stresses of death.

Losing your keys, forgetting to feed the pets, being confused by which day of the week it is, inability to stick with a task, and general indecision are par for the course, and to be expected.

When it happens, please forgive yourself, chuckle, say a few words to yourself, and move on. Most likely, the instant you've released that judgment against yourself, you'll remember what brought you into that room. Do you find that to ring true?

Remember that your subconscious mind has all the answers, all the time. I invite you to welcome your subconscious mind and its understanding and its pure wisdom into your conscious life. Once welcomed in, your subconscious mind will serve you up answer after answer, strategy after strategy.

Yet, if you've been deriding your subconscious mind with statements like, "I can't believe how stupid I am in losing this sock/camera/cell phone, etc.," you may imagine your subconscious mind figuratively cowering in the corner, protecting itself against any further attacks.

As an exercise now, I invite you to speak gently to your subconscious mind, and your being: "I know and trust that you and I have all the answers, [perhaps adding these words, "which are inspired/given by God/our Higher Power"] and I honor that, and I honor you. I thank you for all the answers you have given me today, yesterday, last week, and all the weeks and days and hours of my life. I will continue to seek out and access your power and wisdom as I need it; thank you, thank you, THANK YOU!" Then sit with that silence and soak in the love and empowerment--they are both yours to access and enjoy.

Even if you may have worked in a business career or been very capable with money, you may find your mind blanking out on basic logic questions and mathematical problems. This temporary garbling of the brain's function is completely normal and to be expected (and not judged), since you are bearing the weight of all the decision-making now, regardless of whether you and your late husband made decisions separately or together. Now **you don't have even that choice** of including your husband in the decisions (on this life-plane), so a lot is resting on your shoulders, generally including self-imposed pressures.

In the case that I may have thrown some of my readers off just now, having spoken about "on this life-plane," let me explain what I mean. I fully believe that we CAN continue to evoke our deceased's influence and guidance on matters by simply stating our wishes, concerns or challenges, and addressing our beloved (and in my belief system, God as well), asking them to help guide us in making the very best decisions.

Writing things down on paper or on your computer, or typing words on a smart phone app, or recording your voice which gets transcribed into words on your cell phone app, are all good remedies to lessen your frustration-level, as is maintaining a sense of humor. Positive self-talk may be helpful here, such as, "okay, no problem, I do know how to solve this…okay, keep breathing," etc.

Finally, give yourself permission to change your mind and/or to make sudden plan changes when a different mood strikes you. It's normal and it's okay!

Summary Takeaway:

Too often we berate ourselves for lapsed states of memory; yet they are natural. Dump the self-judgment. Now you have a different perspective on life and it may well be an opportunity to relax some of your earlier-held rules.

After all, your perception of what's important has undergone a seismic shift. Breathe, and notice your feelings as well as your opportunities to release stuff that no longer commands the same meaning in your life.

Honor your husband by saying his name, repeatedly.

Chapter 3
Stupid-Ass Things People Say!

Okay, brace yourself. We can surely excuse a widow's brain from being scrambled with the horrific shock of her husband's death, yet sadly grief seems to also scramble some friends' and families' minds and tongues.

Hearing, and dealing with, stupid-ass comments some friends and family members may make about your late husband's death may exact a LOT of your scant energy and patience, so buck up. I know, it's like a Ripley's Believe It or Not, right? One more thing you have to do, help your friends deal with your grief.

They almost never utter your husband's name. It's a game of "he" and "him" statements, quite often when the sweetest thing your ears could hear would be your husband's name. So, as I said last chapter, just keep saying his name, privately and also with people present.

The befuddlement that strikes your friends, family and acquaintances when they hear of your husband's death often results in their blurting out the absolute stupidest comments in the galaxy, exactly at a time when probably what you most need is a quiet calming voice, a shoulder to lean on, an embrace, an ear to hear you, or silence.

Some of the more common numbnut comments follow:

- It's all for the best.
- Don't you know CPR?
- You brought your kids here?
- If I know him, he left you well off.
- Why didn't you have an open casket?
- You're doing so well; you're strong.
- You're young, you'll remarry.
- Keep busy; time heals everything.
- God needed another angel.
- Now you can go find your soul mate.
- Only the good die young.
- Just get through the first year.
- It's good you had children with him.
- It's good you didn't have children with him.
- I know EXACTLY what you're feeling, my cat died last week.
- I know EXACTLY how you're feeling, my 99 yr. old grandma died last week.
- What was he doing on a motorcycle when you have a two yr. old?
- Don't worry, your son will become the man of the family now.
- I heard you weren't there when he died; it's best that way.

- It's okay, you can sue and get money from the other party.

Most of these comments will be heard in the receiving line at the funeral or memorial service. I don't really have many words of wisdom here, other than to do your best to keep from slapping them on the spot. People generally DO mean well; yet it would help if they would THINK before they speak. Further witness to the fact that our society is still embryonic about comforting grieving people with honor and dignity and respect.

You will invariably have to tell your friends specifically what you need. Do speak up and allow your friends to give to you. And as you begin crying as you are speaking there's no need to say, "I'm sorry." This is another ridiculous adage in our society that people apologize for doing what's perfectly natural when grieving.

Aisle Seven in The Grocery Store

It's also possible to be assaulted with free-floating insensitivity in aisle seven of the grocery store, as a friend speeds by you with her cart--head turned away and not even greeting you--while you stand staring at your husband's favorite cereal on the shelf.

Speaking of aisle seven, be prepared for any of your friends to scurry like young rabbits to a different aisle in the store when they spot you at the other end of the aisle. If that reduces the number of rude comments, all the better, yet seriously, you NEED connection, so it's hurtful. I'm sorry.

Might I suggest your waving at that very friend, so as to let them know that even though you're indeed grieving, you're not blind? You saw them appear, immediately express shock at seeing you, and start to turn away.

One widow client of mine, who became sick and tired of this treatment, even after six months, hollered out, "widow in aisle seven" for all to hear. She then burst out laughing as did all the people around her. I suspect no one in aisle seven that day will ever dodge a widow in the grocery store again.

Luckily most widows report that they don't really remember **what** folks said at the funeral or memorial service; they just remember that there were a lot of supportive people in attendance. Well I can only hope you don't remember the stupid remarks, yet if you do, that you are able to forgive these lame and misguided efforts to be supportive.

Summary Takeaway:

While people do mean well, they often blurt out hurtful comments. Do your best to dismiss their stupidity and appreciate their presence as a sign of support.

Chapter 4
Six Month "No Decision" Zone

While I do outline what you need to do now in Chapter 11, because of the terrific upset that grief produces, I recommend that you avoid making any **major** financial decisions on your own for at least 6 months. Grieving is indeed a full time job. There will be plenty of time to react and to change course after 6 months, perhaps even a year, if that is necessary. I have written Part II of this book to help you do just that, as you are ready.

Relax now from any **major** personal financial decision-making pressure, then, into the space that you deserve to gather yourself and your records. The **decisions that should be avoided for at least 6 months** include, yet are not limited to:

- Buying an annuity or life insurance, regardless of how "nice" the agent appears (See Warnings in Chapters 18 and 38. These two products carry **significant** surrender charges extending 7-10+ years that severely limit your liquidity and cash flow.)

- Selling company stock in a 401(k) retirement plan; there are VERY favorable options for company stock unlike any other subaccount.

- Moving/changing your principal residence
- Remodeling your principal residence
- Buying another home
- Negotiating on anything from car loan/lease rates to mortgage rates, to house sales' prices
- Making significant investment changes
- Liquidating or distributing the assets of the estate (except for paying estate bills)
- If your loved one was cremated, deciding the destination/resting place of his ashes.
- Choosing the proper business form for your new self-employed venture.

These feel like momentous decisions while grief is still new. Yet in a few months' time, you will have a clearer idea of the total landscape--financial and personal--and will be able to focus more clearly on your options. Granted, at first it can appear like there aren't any options at all, or only bleak ones at best, yet in the information gathering process, more options will appear.

Summary Takeaway:

You are regrouping right now, and will make more clear-headed decisions on large items with a few more tools and a lot more information that you will assimilate over time. **Chapter 11 outlines what you need to do now.**

Chapter 5
Emoting Fully in Safe Places

While it's just plain smart to seek out and find safe places to release emotions, it is also vital to cry whenever the tears arrive. It's been said that "tears are a shower for the soul." Crying is not only okay, it's essential for healing. If you can't feel it, you can't heal it.

If you begin to cry when you are with someone, just finish your tears, maybe putting up a forefinger, so as to indicate, wait a minute please. There is no need to apologize for crying by saying, "I'm sorry." Rather people will expect you to cry since crying is a healthy response to grief and missing your beloved.

Your funeral home director, pastor, rabbi or priest can generally provide recommendations of different local grief groups. More recently, with the Internet providing ready communication and instant search access, grief groups have sprung up to support survivors whose partners died of either specific illnesses or incidents--cancer, diabetes, AIDS, heart attacks, auto/plane/bike accidents, suicide, murder or wrongful death.

While these similar-circumstances-of-death grief recovery groups often sound like great choices; i.e., providing like-situation people an atmosphere in which to share, I also know that grieving survivors of a similar incident ultimately may or may not be compatible. For example, a widow whose husband died of lung cancer having never smoked a day in his life, may **not** find a kindred soul within a group of widows whose husbands also died of lung cancer, yet had smoked for decades. Sometimes these survivors make strange bedfellows.

If you are a young widow, or a young widow with children, you will face different challenges than those of an older widow, for example; so seek out a group that is age-relative. Just the presence of one other widow, let alone several, who have moved through situations that you are just now facing can serve as a beacon of hope that you, too, can do this. Yes you can.

The important factor is to attend a couple of local meetings of a group to get a feeling for the type of people involved. If you don't feel comfortable in that group, continue your sampling of groups until you find one that fits. We women are typically great shoppers, continuing our search until we find the exact pair of shoes and so forth. No different with grief groups; it's vital to find people with whom you feel comfortable.

Additionally (and I know I'm on thin ice here) if the same attendees are reciting their story for the umpteenth time, seemingly stuck in the effect of their pain or their circumstances, you will want to seek out a group in which people's stories are told and valued, after which forward progress is encouraged.

As in all of life, there are folks who, for myriad reasons, get stuck in the recitation of the event/loss rather than risk taking baby steps of courage to move a little bit further through their past into their present. At some point widows realize the futility of wishing for a different past, and slowly embark on exploring and creating their "now."

You will learn quickly which friends and family members can sit with you (or receive a phone call from you) to listen to you cry, without feeling the urge to *fix* you. Your therapist or grief coach are two other dependable resources that will be professionally trained to counsel or coach you through particularly rough waters.

Thousands of widows and widowers have also come to call Camp Widow® weekends home due to the camaraderie and kinship engendered amongst women and men who have lost their life partner. Camp Widow® was established by Michele Neff Hernandez, a widow who also created Soaring Spirits to "make a difference for widowed people around the world."

Michele felt passionately that widows and widowers needed the opportunity to gather together, at least annually, to share stories, tears and laughter. She has indeed created safe space at Camp Widow East, Camp Widow West, as well as Camp Widow Toronto.

These weekends provide widows the unique experience of being in the majority rather than feeling isolated, as they often feel in other social settings. Widows and widowers experience bonding space, grieving space, space to laugh and dance. They also learn new opportunities in the informative educational workshops interspersed throughout the weekend. Peer-based encouragement abounds, buoying widows' hope and mustering their courage to face the next wave of rebuilding their lives.

I have every confidence that Michele will continue to expand the myriad services and outreach of both Camp Widow and Soaring Spirits. Stay tuned at www.CampWidow.org and www.SoaringSpirits.org.

Summary Takeaway:

While it's indeed vital to cry whenever your emotions well up, it is wise to seek certifiably safe spaces in order to ensure full acceptance of your tears and vulnerabilities.

Chapter 6
I Need a Good Listening To!

My dear friend and widow, Abby, shared with me the need for widows to sometimes "barf up the whole story" to anyone at any time initially in the grief process. However, she assured me that eventually widows discern when and where this may be appropriate.

Sometimes a widow knows when she needs or wants to talk, yet sometimes she may not. The swirl of emotions--those temporarily in check and those that gyrate actively right beneath the surface--often splash up against each other, producing a great deal of uncertainty as to whether talking may be helpful or not. And sometimes, without any warning whatsoever, talking will seem like the last thing a widow wants to do, even after having started a sentence. If you're that widow, forgive yourself, it's okay.

In 2009 I interviewed Dr. Ted Klontz, a Clinical Licensed Psychologist with extensive experience working with people's money problems and emotions. He is a soft-spoken yet confident man whom I find to be incredibly wise. We shared stories of working with widowed clients, nodding in agreement as each of us detailed the particulars of their healing journeys. Suddenly he stopped mid-sentence and leaned forward towards me, wagging his forefinger. He asked, "Debra, do you know what people **need** today?" My mind raced to find the answer--running the gamut from a job, to better communication, to more money, to sex, etc.,--then I replied, "No, I don't know what people need today." He quietly responded, **"A good LISTENING to!"**

His answer completely floored me, since a wagging forefinger has almost always held a fist full of condemnation for me in the past. I took in his response so entirely that my body froze in time, just to comprehend the profundity of that wisdom. I was, and am, forever changed. Since then, **I champion the art of listening** and work towards being a better listener.

Widows especially need good listeners, people who will "listen them into speech" as my dear friend Dr. Virginia Mollenkott wrote in her book, *Speech, Silence, Action! The Cycle of Faith,* published by Abingdon Press in 1980. It's after speaking that wise folk grow silent, and then create viable action steps, until the cycle repeats itself.

In a society where many talk less and less, abbreviate words and use emoticons in text messages, I urge us to resurrect the fine art of listening, and, of course, speaking.

Summary Takeaway:

Upon finding a good listener, speak your truths and feel the corresponding relief.

Chapter 7
Would a Grief Coach Help?

What's a grief coach, and do you need or want one?

Thankfully this profession has risen into prominence during the last decade, to lend support to the ever growing number of widows and widowers. Separate and apart from psychotherapists and psychiatrists, grief coaches are trained with proven strategies to shorten the time of fully processing and moving through grief.

The January 17, 2005 *Time* Magazine featured an article entitled, *The New Science of HAPPINESS* stating that "it takes five to eight years for a widow to regain her previous sense of well-being." Many such articles on grief state that *it just takes time*, implying that time alone heals.

If it just took time, everyone who had lost a spouse 3-10 years ago, or longer, would be totally through their grieving process and moving forward in the knowledge and eventual comfort of their own completeness, living meaningful and productive lives. Yet, sadly, many are not. Or at least not enough of them have navigated through their grief to the extent that that they can now enjoy loving and joyous memories of their husband without retreating into silence or remorse-filled isolation.

Time alone does not heal a grieving heart any more than time alone heals a broken tibia bone. We all know the routine if we break our leg. We go to the hospital to get our leg bone set and stabilized in a cast, and we're forbidden from putting weight on it to allow healing over 6 to 8 weeks.

Similarly, strategies and specific actions can significantly lessen the amount of time it takes for a person to move through the painful chasm of grief and emerge on the other side, feeling whole again. I didn't say afflicted with amnesia or denial; I said "whole"--complete within oneself, with full access to memories and a range of emotions.

A grief coach can also empathize with and strategize to handle awkward situations. For instance when the dinner check comes, do you hand over cash or a credit card for the price of your dinner, or graciously accept the offer of the inviting couple? While the latter may be fine the first time, if there is a second dinner gathering, what is protocol, and how can delicate situations be handled with ease?

On that topic of dining invitations, I prepare my widow coaching clients that typically widows are invited only ONCE by their couple friends. It's sad yet true that apparently couples assuage their discomfort by a single invitation, yet seemingly are too uncomfortable to make a second invitation.

Knowing that fact in advance helps protect my clients' self-esteem, since it isn't about them; it's just a very sad and pathetic pattern. Widows who are aware of the pattern don't suffer so much hurt and confusion about being abandoned by their familiar social network, in addition to losing their partner. No one needs this double whammy.

Additionally, if folks you are around speak to you in words such as, "at least it wasn't..." or "sorry he lost the battle with X illness" you may wish to tune out, as these are yet more examples of insensitive comments.

A Certified Grief Coach trained specifically in grief recovery will listen to you, will help elicit consciousness about your fears, and will help to understand your situation in order to tailor-design a plan of how best to proceed, all the while giving you the needed space and support to grieve.

John W. James and Russell Friedman founded The Grief Recovery Institute, co-authoring *The Grief Recovery Handbook* and *Moving On*. For a grief coach referral, see: www.griefrecoverymethod.com/outreach-program.

In my Grief Coach Academy Certification process, I learned myriad strategies that dovetail with my financial training to provide clients a profound and empowering financial lifeline. I find it most fulfilling to rekindle the hope in widows' eyes and be an agent to their processing their grief more swiftly.

If you have a child or children, their grieving needs may be best met by engaging them to talk about their feelings, as well as connecting them with particular professional services tailored to healing sibling loss. Imagine, A Center For Coping With Loss (www.Imaginenj.org) was founded by Mary Robinson, who suffered the death of her dad when she was 14 years old.

Mary speaks of receiving a cherished note from her neighbor, which validated both Mary and her loss; something folks too often forget to tell children.

My friend, Zander Sprague's 30-year old sister was murdered when he was 28. He authored *Making Lemonade: Choosing a Positive Pathway After Losing Your Sibling* to serve as a resource to grieving siblings. Dr. Christina Hibbert buried 2 young sisters; see her many resources at www.drchristinahibbert.com.

It is surprising to hear that kids are asked how their mom is doing, yet seldom asked how **they** are doing. All the while most kids are focused on their mom, sometimes to the exclusion of expressing their own feelings.

Summary Takeaway:

A Certified Grief Coach can provide safe space. Grief coaches are trained to listen without attempting to fix, and to offer you (and/or children) strategy steps only when you are ready for them. Kids need noticed and their loss both validated and healed too.

Chapter 8
Angelversaries, Holidays & Sex

I know: HOW in the world did I put these topics together? Well, it seemed to make sense to me, yet you'll be the ultimate judge.

The first year of grief is so **very** difficult because of the number of firsts without your love--first birthdays, first anniversaries and the first set of holidays as a widow.

You may find comfort in referring to these dates as Angelversaries. These dates will always remain special, and you will remember them however is best for you. Many find comfort in the thought or belief that their beloved is also tuned into these dates, much like that of an angel's presence; hence the term Angelversaries.

Many women continue to buy greeting cards to commemorate these days. They open and read the card aloud to their beloved, or on your birthday to yourself, and sit in silence to receive whatever comfort, tears or joy that may come.

Be ever so gentle with yourself on these days, they will get easier after each of the *firsts*.

Weddings
I advise that you respectfully decline wedding invitations in the first year if possible, as the sight of two people celebrating the

beginning of what they believe will be a long lifetime together will hit you like a ton of bricks. That's how YOU felt, too! And it got cut terribly short; it's not fair.

It's excruciatingly painful to remember your own wedding day, as most folks do when they attend weddings. All the anticipation, and then the day arrived and everything worked. Or what didn't work was fodder for funny stories ever since. Yet now, you're a witness to someone else's dream day of uniting with the one they've chosen. And the energy you have to muster not to cry is enormous.

Generally folks don't want to see someone crying out of sadness and loss at a wedding, so the cost of bottling up your feelings and suppressing very natural tears is most likely too high a price to pay.

IF, however, it is a family wedding which you cannot skip, then simply write to the bride and groom saying that you are so very happy for them, and to interpret your tears--when they well up and spill out onto your cheeks--as your remembrance of your celebration of love. Remind them to treat each other as if each day counts, because it does. This may be the best and most meaningful wedding present they will receive; words of wisdom about the fragility of time.

Schedule a meet-up with a friend, or better yet have the friend come to your home after the wedding, so you can just bawl, or be held. Weddings are so very tough.

Blog Advice

Read any of the widow blogs and/or search the Internet for suggestions as to how to commemorate each of the formerly special dates with your husband so that you have a plan ahead of time. While some women prefer solitude, others arrange to be with friends.

Often birthdays and major holidays are spent with family and friends, unlike wedding anniversaries, which had generally been celebrated more privately. The balancing act of which family you choose to be with on each of these holidays is just that, a balancing act. When you are invited, thank the inviter and take some time to consider the invitation. There's no need to answer right away, nor harm in changing your mind later.

We can't predict who will offer comfort on these days, or in these seasons. Sometimes family members who we counted upon in the past, have an allergy to mentioning your husband's name. You will either call them out on that, insisting that he be mentioned by name during the conversations, or you will choose different company. Or you will choose to be alone, yet I caution you to have a back-up plan if you do, in case it gets to feeling too lonely.

Many widows plan "bookend events" with friends and family, allowing a ½ day between those events for solitude. This combination may prove to strike the right balance.

Avoid the Empty Calendar Syndrome

Looking at an empty calendar for October, November & December is downright depressing, so do pencil some activities in; you can always change your mind later. Plus the act of writing in activities or trips with people you'd like to see will give you time to really think about these, and determine whether the feeling is still right a week or two after initially writing it down.

Some widows write to family and friends whom they will be meeting with, requesting that everyone maintain flexibility around the festivities, repeating many or all traditions, while also recognizing that "there is one less of us this day" with some time for silence and reflection-- tears and/or funny stories.

Many widows plan to travel to another destination for the first holidays, allowing them new experiences to see and feel, to balance out the tremendous feelings of loss of their beloved.

Flying on Thanksgiving or Christmas day can be very reasonably priced, I've noticed. So, if you plan on getting away, you may consider this cost saver. While the flight attendants will surely be happier, they have a specific job to do that day--ensuring your safety until you get to your final destination--and they will attend to that yet also allow you some privacy. Family gatherings, on the other hand, have no other purpose than to *be* together, perhaps the very activity you would rather avoid.

While no one will argue that these are incredibly difficult times/weekends/weeks, I invite you to lock onto children's joy at Christmas or Hanukkah, insomuch as their innocence is tender and perhaps heartwarming. They don't know, nor can they understand your grief; ultimately it's all about them and their presents. So go there with them, and celebrate their happiness.

If you can look for some joy to assuage your sadness then you will usher in healing a little bit sooner. It will be easier the second and third years; it will.

Ordering in Chinese or Thai food and watching senseless TV or a movie, preferably a light comedy, or a travel movie, or a National Geographic type of show can take your mind off the constant jangle of Christmas or Hanukkah, even for a couple of hours.

Google the Internet for singles groups and widowed groups that gather during the major holidays and pry yourself out of your home to attend one or two. The new scenery may well be healing.

Giving Is Healing

Finally, make it a point to give to someone. The act of giving is one of the single most healing activities, if even only a smile to the toll taker, or check-out clerk, or to the grocery bagger, or to the mail delivery person.

And buy yourself a small present for special occasions, something you would have asked him to buy for you. Or find or buy a special small trinket that you can carry in your pocket to remind yourself of his presence and his love.

Giving physical gifts may not appeal to you, yet if it does, shop via catalog so as to avoid all the holiday *cheer* and unruly crowds at the malls.

The Monday after Thanksgiving is generally the best day to buy gifts online, as most companies offer free shipping and generous discounts. Obviously some retailers offer huge discounts on the Friday after Thanksgiving, otherwise referred to as Black Friday. Shopping online can save you a lot of grief of having to come face-to-face with scant parking, potentially horrid wintery weather, rude shoppers or store clerks and those endless holiday tunes and decorations.

You can even buy your holiday wrapping paper online, or use up what's left from last year to avoid having to make yet more choices during a time of extra stress.

My best suggestion is to limit the number of choices you need to make. Limit the number of personal encounters you have to make. And choose those you would like to visit/see during the holidays, and make plans well in advance to do just that.

Consider preparing a shoebox of gifts for a soldier or kid in a developing country as your holiday gift-giving focus. Many community groups or religious groups will collect (typically unwrapped) gifts for distribution to others. This can give you a rich feeling of gift-giving, without needing to be in relationship with the receiver.

WWMHD?

Ultimately you need to make decisions that feel right to you on these Angelversaries. If you have no clue, I invite you to think about what would your husband do? How would your husband want you to feel on your birthday, Halloween, his Birthday, Thanksgiving, Christmas, Hanukkah, New Year's, Easter, Memorial Day, 4th of July, Labor Day, Columbus Day, and the like?

Rather than feeling guilty about any small celebration on these days, (as if that could signal to your beloved or anyone else close enough to notice, that you didn't love him, and aren't grieving his loss *enough*) go ahead and imagine what he would suggest and do that.

Other Firsts

A warning about New Year's is in order. This holiday is so often followed by a significant hangover for those who drink, it's best to avoid the drinking and the hangover. So much of the hype is to sell overpriced tickets to dance venues for couples, I say steer clear. If you must watch the ball drop, do so from your bed or sofa, not jammed into some noisy, cramped ball room or bar.

The anniversary of your husband's death will no doubt be the quintessential horrible angelversary. On the one hand, it'll evoke the memory of "the moment" of his death, or your notification of his death. On the other hand, while it will also signal that you've just survived potentially the single worst year of your life, you can know, or believe, that it can only get easier going forward.

"Doing" angelversaries with children, especially young children, is an extra challenge, simply because children don't process grief as do adults. Children may well react hugely on let's say the 3rd angelversary. You may well wonder why then, yet ultimately, no one has a recipe for grief reactions; they come when they come and, as such, they should be expressed and felt. If you can encourage your kid(s) to talk as they emote, it will clue you into the genesis of their emotions and perhaps the reason for the intensity; not that there has to be a rational reason, mind you, yet it will be interesting to note.

Sexual (Or Other) Release

While this may vary depending upon your age, often widows wracked with hurt/anger/frustration feel certain urges to find a physical release for their pent up emotions. And why not? It is perfectly natural and a sign of strength for you to begin to chip away at the dam that was built around the flood of your emotions.

This release may take the form of a hike or other physical exercise, or it may be best assuaged by having sex. Not loving, romantic sex; long, hard and exhausting sex. While there are plenty of men who will be willing to oblige, caution is in order here. First, avoid having sex with married men. If they aren't willing to give you their phone number, or to receive calls from you at dinner time or later, that may be a clue that they aren't as unmarried as they attest.

Divorced or widowed men do exist who may be in a similar situation to yours, yet finding them could be challenging. Meet-up groups for singles or widowed people may be valuable resources. Yet be certain to state up front exactly what you are seeking: sex to temporarily release tension, stress, hurt, sadness, anger, whatever. You are NOT looking for a relationship at this point.

An obvious alternative to sex with a man would be to use a vibrator or other sex toy, which can be purchased online from any number of vendors. Here's one such vendor: www.pureromance.com/shop/Adult-Sex-Toys/For-Women.

Be sure, however, to Google search for any sex-toys under a **private** Internet search window only; else you will be barraged by ongoing pop-up ads and unwanted emails for the rest of your life. To get to a private search window, just follow the directions of whichever browser you are using. Just type into the search bar, "how do I access a private search window?" and follow those directions carefully. Once you are actually on a private search window, you will see an image in either the top right or left corner of your screen. Mine is like a small theater mask image. Without that, you aren't in a private search window, so go back and try again.

I have a private search bar bookmarked on my computer, as I prefer to search for what I'm looking for without "cookies" attaching themselves to what I'm searching for.

Incidentally, sex aside, it has been proven that certain airlines and car rental agencies capture your Internet search criteria, and then the next time you access their site to make your purchase, the price is higher! They know you are interested, so they feel justified in charging you more if you go back to that site. So, I prefer to use the private search feature a LOT, as it maintains my privacy, alleviates a ton of junk on my computer, and saves me paying these Internet crawler's increased prices.

Summary Takeaway:

In any event, each angelversary is followed by a non-angelversary day, an ordinary day on the calendar. So just get through one day at a time, however you need to do it.

Chapter 9
What to Do With His Stuff?

Each widow invariably knows her timeline with regard to what to do with all his stuff: his pictures, his wallet, his clothes, his shoes, his sports equipment, his car, his bicycle, his collections, his cologne--his stuff. It's everywhere. It was part of his life and now that he's died, it's part of your life.

Sometimes you'll feel comforted looking at it, sometimes you'll feel crushed and excruciatingly sad or angry looking at it, handling it, and fondling it. Some of it you'll keep and use as a loving reminder of him, some of it you'll give to family or friends who will also treasure having something to remember him by. And some of it you'll give to charity, to pay it forward.

I've coached widows whose husbands died suddenly who acted very swiftly to give away their husband's stuff under the guise that if they didn't see their husband's belongings everywhere they turned, they would feel better. Actually, so as not to risk feeling regret later, it's best to take all the time you need.

While family and friends do tend to immediately swarm into your home to keep you company and support you, tell one person whom you will put in charge to advise that no one touches the laundry or any of your husband's stuff.

This will allow you to smell his scent on his clothes for days and weeks, while it lingers, and wear his clothes to comfort you.

Realizing that your energy is at a premium, leave this sorting until later when a friend or family member can help you divide things into boxes with specific people's names on them and boxes for charity and boxes for the "I can't decide yet what to do with these items," of which there will be many. This is a process which may occur in stages; in 6 months you can pull out the "I can't decide what to do with these items" boxes and have more clarity. Or not.

My friend and grief coaching colleague, Colleen, describes finally being ready to take Rod's clothes from his closet only to have her kids hang everything back on hangers, re-filling his closet. Clearly emotions run deep and everyone has an opinion, yet your opinion and your timing trumps everyone else's. Colleen was able to talk with her children and eventually they gave her the space and freedom to sort through Rod's closets.

She and a quilter made 4 beautiful quilts out of Rod's clothing and gifted each of her kids their own quilt of Rod's sweatshirts, pants and tee-shirts the following Christmas. Clearly her kids were moved to be able to treasure their dad's clothes in a quilt which served also as a comforting wrap on Christmas day and every day. They were literally wrapped up in Rod's and Colleen's love for them.

Another friend made a round tablecloth by sewing together her husband's neck ties. It was beautiful enough to frame and hang, so she decided to do that, and then made another for her small deck table where she has coffee each morning.

Many widows make collages of certain of their husband's belongings--driver's license, marriage certificate, newspaper obituary, vacation photos, sweet notes, passport, professional designation certificates, press releases and hobby fare. These collages may be themed and named as such, and hung in various rooms of your home as loving reminders of the valuable and precious time you shared. Celebrate your love. Although it was cut short on this earth plane, it was genuine and rare.

Often family and friends will collect and present photos to you for the memorial service. Even after the service, ask folks to pass along their pictures to you, or their videos of your husband, so you can view them whenever you'd like. Often family and friends will make a DVD or a CD which is a heart-warming gift that you'll cherish forever. Or you can make one, or ask a friend to help you make one, after you get more photos collected.

Journaling about what you most loved about your husband may dovetail into making a collage about those things. Conversely, listing some of your pet peeves may also be fodder for a collage; one that you will smirk at or roll your eyes at each time you see it. Celebrate his humanness and your humanness. He'll get a kick out of it too, just ask him. You'll see.

Summary Takeaway:

Sorting through your husband's stuff will be an emotional yet healing step in grieving his loss. You'll keep many things as reminders of him and give some of his treasured belongings to your family and friends. Take your time with this step; there's no hurry.

Chapter 10
Unwinding Emotions & Money

Money and emotions are inextricably connected. And I could well understand if money is the last thing you want to think about now. Yet if your ignorance about money is a big part of the weight you bear, it makes sense to lighten that load sooner rather than later.

While you have friends and family to support you emotionally, you may find yourself less able to quell your late night--or heck, perhaps 24 hour--worries about money.

One of our first tasks is to unwind emotions and money from their tight knot. Money isn't to be loved or hated; money is simply a **tool**.

I invite you now to re-imagine money as currency to buy choices--now and in the future. You've just survived a **major** stress, and you deserve choices. You deserve options to help you move through this gnarly unknown.

"Easy for you to say," you may want to retort! Yes, it very well may be easier for me, principally because I have seen money buy widows choices thousands of times. WhatEVER amount of money you have now is what we'll work with to maximize your choices. If that amount isn't enough to last for your lifetime, we'll strategize your options to change that.

Part I of this book is my attempt to help you understand the appropriate context for your relationship with money from this day forward, and to help you create new money messages. In my 36+ years as a financial planner, I've never met a money problem that was unsolvable.

It's imperative, however, to understand that historical references to money have been particularly negative for women. For example, what did you hear growing up? Do any of these sound familiar?

- Money is filthy lucre,
- Money won't buy you happiness,
- Money is the root of all evil,
- Money and a fool are quickly parted, or
- Money is unmentionable in polite society.

Yet curiously men were taught (and all successful people believe) money will buy choices about:

- Where I will live,
- Where I send my children to school or college,
- How long I can stay out of the workforce,
- Whether I can switch from full-time to part-time,

- Whether I can afford to retire before age 70, or not,

- What type or frequency of vacations I can take,

- How much I can spend on my lifestyle, or,

- How much I can plan on spending later.

What a difference such choices make!

Now write down--just free associate here please--what societal money messages you remember hearing as you were both a young girl, then an adolescent, then a young woman, and so on:

_____

_____

_____

_____

Depending on your age, the social messages will vary, based upon the societal roles women have been expected to assume. Regardless, men's money messages were/are powerful and life-giving, and women's usually were not.

I think it's empowering to notice that our environment is responsible for some of women's free-floating anxiety about money. It's not our fault we weren't taught better! Regardless, we have some catching up to do, and together, We Can Do It Women!™

While **family** money messages reflect society's messages, they have a different flair--again, often more searing for women. "Don't worry your little head over that, your husband will handle the money" rings all too familiar in many families.

Now write down either what your parents said about money, or what you came to understand about money and women's role toward money:

———————————————————

———————————————————

———————————————————

———————————————————

Clearly, you married and you assumed the role of *wife* with all that role meant in your family, and now he's gone, perhaps before you had learned just what it was that he did with your money all those years.

You have every right to feel doubly poor. First, at his passing, you have instantly lost your respectable *wife* status, and second, **you** are now responsible for a whole other universe than that which you may be comfortable managing. Neither of these are small matters. Both have to be vetted, talked about, and, in time, accepted. As such, I am committed to giving women the tools to replace those negative and just plain false axioms with more empowered money statements.

If money can provide all these choices that men were taught, how can those old societal or familial negative messages really make sense? You're right, they don't. Money is a tool that creates possibilities for all genders.

I can't help myself from offering analogies here. If I asked you to make a dinner entrée, yet gave you only ½ the necessary ingredients, you'd have to adjust either the entrée you're making, or the size of it. Or you may go borrow or buy some ingredients to achieve the goal of making dinner. You would adapt somehow because you are a woman. Will the entrée be as good as it could have been with all the ingredients? No. Will it be edible and satisfying? Most likely.

Similarly, if a golfer shows up to play a round of golf at the course with only 8 clubs in her bag instead of the maximum allowable 14 clubs, she'll have to make some adjustments in her game. Not having the 4 iron, for example, could potentially cause her to have to take one more hit (or stroke) on a long hole. Will she finish that round of golf? Yes. Will she score as well as if she had used 12 or 14 clubs? Nope.

Whether they take the form of ingredients, golf clubs or money in these examples, tools are just that: tools. The right tools always make any job easier, so let's not waste time or opportunity. Instead, let's identify and grow comfortable with our next financial steps.

Ask yourself, "what is my future (and possibly that of my kids) going to look and feel like, if I ignore money matters for another two years?" compared to "what is my future going to look and feel like if I use this time and opportunity to take control of both saving and spending right here, right now?"

The price tag of waiting any longer to take control of your finances could be extreme, due to the power of compounding working **against** you. Additionally, the personal stress of worrying about uncertainty any longer could take an additional and undue toll on your physical and mental health.

All signs point to the lasting benefits of our doing some serious fact-finding, followed by tempered and deliberate baby action steps.

We will rid ourselves of inaction and any free-floating anxiety about money--it's most likely NOT as dire as you fear, yet should it be, we can begin to deal with next steps sooner rather than later.

Will you finish life with the money you have now and the future money you will earn or possibly inherit? Yes. Will your life be easier if you not only maintain but grow the money you have now as well as grow your future investments until you need them? Yes.

I will provide strategies to become more enlightened/empowered, which is as much a process of un-learning for most women as it is acquiring new skills, due to those negative familial or societal money messages.

Since knowledge is power, I've included a glossary of what I deem to be important financial terms at the back of this book, along with my definitions in plain English (not financese). So feel free to peruse those when you don't know the meaning of a term you may be reading.

As Oprah Winfrey and others are fond of saying, you have ALL the answers within you! With some coaching from professionals and trusted friends, you will create an empowered "new you" and a profitable future.

I can also appreciate that this prophecy may either hit you as insensitive on my part, or simply a state you can't even imagine now. Either is understandable and okay, and I invite you to keep reading.

Summary Takeaway:

In this very new chapter of you, like a phoenix, you will acknowledge and release your old money messages, in favor of new attitudes about the tool called money and the freedom and choices it will buy for you.

Chapter 11
Important Notifications to Make

You will need to notify your Attorney, Financial Planner, Life Insurance Agent, your husband's former Employer(s), Social Security, and Credit Card Companies as soon as you are able to reach out to them. Details follow:

Estate Settlement Attorney

If you have an attorney who prepared your late husband's will, call that person and inform them of the death. If you have a copy of your husband's will, read through it ahead of your appointment to meet with your attorney. Perhaps make a copy of the will so you can write directly onto the pages, or highlight portions that need clarification. Alternatively, if you can't make a copy of the will, either write on the pages in pencil or simply write down every question you have on a note pad, so that you can get these specific questions answered.

If your late husband did NOT sign his will, the state in which he resided has a substitute will for him, and the assets will be disbursed according to what is called the Law of Intestacy: i.e., dying without a will. These vary between states, so research this at your library or on the Internet as to what that entails. If they have not otherwise been exempted--passing directly via a beneficiary designation or owned by certain types of trusts for example--your late husband's assets will pass through a process called probate.

I recommend that you ask your funeral director for the names of a few reputable estate distribution/settlement attorneys, or check the website of your town's estate planner councils for people with whom you will arrange an appointment to discuss the required next steps for settling the estate. If the attorney who prepared the will is an estate planning attorney, you can of course work with her or him.

Steer clear of your friend, or the real estate attorney that closed on your home or refinanced your mortgage. Because estate settlement is an ever-changing field of law, you do NOT want to make costly mistakes. You should no more meet with an attorney who does not specialize in estate settlement or estate planning than you would engage a podiatrist for inner ear surgery; both are doctors, yet they serve different ends (specialties, of course; pun intended).

Financial Advisor

If you had been working with a financial advisor, call that person and inform them of the death, and ask them to prepare a written summary overview page of the decedent's assets (decedent is the fancy word for your beloved who has died).

In addition to the list of assets, ask the advisor to write a summarizing statement explaining the type of each investment, the current value, the current loss, if any, on each investment presuming it would be sold at once, and whether there may have been any *accelerated death benefit* over and above the account value, such as an annuity with an enhanced death benefit rider.

Once that WRITTEN asset and explanation statement is prepared, ask the advisor to **mail it to you by US snail mail. This is important; please take note!** Even if you do use email, this information is FAR too personal to entrust to an email transmission. I urge you to adopt this as your overarching guideline about transmitting information through email. If you wouldn't write it on a postcard and mail it, don't send it through regular, unprotected email.

If you prefer using electronic mail, you can purchase any number of computer programs (I use WinZip) for either Personal Computers or Apple/MAC users that will enable you to encrypt and password-protect sensitive documents.

You do NOT want to meet with your current financial agent before you have had ample time to personally review this summary report. I advise that you read the report a couple of times so that you can get familiar with the basics, and then highlight the portions that you may not understand, or write your questions in the margins.

In the next chapter I will explain the differences in financial planners so that you can make an educated decision about which type of financial planner you will eventually meet with to overview this information.

For now, you are gathering the information for your personal review only. You are resisting any requests for a face-to-face meeting until this written report is sent to you and you've had some time to review it, along with the content of the next chapter.

There are three reasons for this advice:

1. You want to have a chance to completely read what's been sent and make a list of questions (remembering that there are no dumb questions). It's your money; ask whatever may be unclear to you. You have every right (and responsibility) to know.

2. You'll want to wait for at least a month after you've completed your organizational tasks, so that you have a more complete assessment of the amounts you may owe, and to whom, and how often--monthly, quarterly or annually.

3. The sale or retitling of various assets, including your husband's IRA and 401(k), or even garden-variety stocks/bonds and mutual funds are complex decisions that require thoughtful consideration, both from an investment and income tax standpoint.

Some of these decisions are irrevocable. Take the proper time and advice from a fee-only CFP® and/or your CPA and/or your attorney to make certain of your choice(s). You may live many decades with the consequences of poor choices. (Sadly, I've inherited a few clients whose agent sold them into products that were irreversible and cost a lot of money. See Chapter 18 now for details, so you'll be fore-warned when "nice/kind" agents approach you, offering to "help.")

Life Insurance Agent(s) if no Financial Advisor

If you are working with a financial advisor, they can provide you all the information on options to receive the death benefit(s), etc., and that information will be included in the financial advisor's packet to you.

If you are not working with a financial advisor, and believe there is a current life insurance contract(s) in force, call the agent who is listed on the statements, or call the main number of the Home Office of the Insurance Company who underwrote the contract(s). The number will be written on the policy, or available via telephone directory assistance or via an Internet search.

For the reasons I've just stated, you will inform them of your husband's death, and ask them to mail you via US Postal service the paperwork you will need to complete, along with the total amount of death benefit payable to you, presuming you were the last named beneficiary.

While the agent will have a vested financial interest in meeting with you, as they see these check-delivering meetings as sales opportunities, please adhere to my advice to have them mail you the information which you can then review with your other professionals, including the CFP® you will research and hire as well as your CPA.

Info to Gather Before Calling Employer

If your husband had ever worked outside the home, he would have received a pay stub, either attached to his check, or in a separate US mailing, or via emailing if his check was auto deposited to a bank account. If you can locate any of these pay stubs, you will see a list of deductions from his pay. You'll see a gross income, and then myriad taxes withdrawn-- numbers with minus signs before them--and possibly any number of deductions labeled life insurance, or long-term care insurance, or pension/401(k)/403(b) contributions. Now you know some of the specific benefits that he paid extra for, in addition to any free group benefits. I will list and define some potential major employer-provided benefits, so read through these sub-headings before you call your husband's employer(s).

Health/Medigap Insurance

Ask his most recent employer what the current laws are related to extended health insurance (otherwise known as COBRA), so that you may continue being covered by your late husband's health insurance. (If your late husband was over age 65, he may have carried an insurance policy called Medigap, which is exactly what it sounds like; it provides potential coverage for charges that Medicare denies. Inquire about the amount it will cost monthly (otherwise known as monthly premium) for coverage on you and on any dependent children, even college-aged children.

The rules tend to change on dependent coverage, so ensure that you have the latest information. Otherwise, if your college-aged children would NOT be covered under your late husband's COBRA, you may have to take out a new health insurance policy for your children. If this is the case, you should call their college, because some colleges offer group insurance rates that are generally less expensive.

To ensure there is no lapse in coverage make sure to determine whether you will mail your monthly premium for continued health or Medigap insurance to the most recent employer, or directly to the health insurance provider.

Because health insurance is so vital, I recommend paying an extra monthly payment so that you are always paid a month in advance. This gives you some additional peace of mind in the case you may forget to pay a monthly premium. Better yet, arrange for the monthly insurance premium payment to be deducted automatically from your credit card, to 1) ensure systematic and on-time payment and 2) earn frequent flier or bonus miles from your credit card company. Alternatively, if the insurance company does not accept credit cards, set up an automatic payment plan directly from your bank or investment brokerage account. The more essential payments you can set on auto pay at this point, the better!

Group Life & Accidental Death Insurance

Ask the supervisor of the human resources department if your late husband may have been covered by any group life insurance contracts-- most likely offered as company fringe benefits.

Often group life insurance is issued as a multiple of one's salary; i.e., death benefit equal to one times salary, or two times salary. Generally it is offered at no charge to the employee. So, if you found his paystub and there are no deductions for life insurance, he STILL may have had group life insurance--on which the premiums were paid on his behalf by the company.

Also ask if he carried any separate, additional life insurance coverage on himself, and possibly you and/or children. (If you were able to find one of his paystubs you can see whether or not he was paying any premiums for either.)

If there is additional group life insurance on you or your child(ren), simply pay the next monthly or quarterly premium just to buy yourself time, and then discuss this with your personal financial planner when you meet. This coverage may or may not be viable to maintain. It all depends on your insurability or that of your child(ren). Because group insurance can be converted to permanent insurance without a medical exam, it could prove invaluable.

Group Long-Term Care Insurance

Your late husband may have been paying premiums on a policy on himself, or both of you, for long-term care. If applicable, determine if there was a death benefit payable on his policy, and inquire about how to continue your own policy. It's very important not to have any lapse in premium for this type of coverage. Typically group policies for long-term care are less expensive than buying an individual long-term care policy. So regardless of whether your late husband had elected it earlier or not, be sure to ask if it may be available to you now.

Calling the Former Employer(s)

As you call your husband's former employer(s), to avert getting incorrect information or sustaining unnecessary delays, ask to speak directly to the supervisor in the human resource department or benefits division. Identify yourself, inform them of your husband's death, and ask them what benefits you may be eligible to receive, noting whatever proofs of insurances he carried if you were able to locate his paystub(s). Ask the supervisor approximately how many death certificates you will need to settle your husband's affairs. Request that you be mailed any and all information including any claim forms requisite to receiving said benefits, via the US Postal (snail) mail, for your analysis and review.

Inform them you will make a second call to them to arrange for a face-to-face interview once you've had adequate time to review the information they send you. Your professionals will assist you in completing all these forms prior to that meeting, no worries. You are simply getting the process started with this initial call and requests.

If your husband had office keys, a parking pass, a company credit/debit card or any other property that could be returned to his employer, gather it up and take it with you to the appointment. If he had an office at his job or career, ask to speak with your husband's boss or department head in order to schedule a date and time for you to meet them to clean out his office.

You will want to take a hand truck, a couple of liquor boxes (they're the strongest), a supportive friend, and several tissues, because this office cleaning will most likely be an emotional experience. As such, I recommend scheduling your visit preferably before or after regular work hours, so as not to meet up with gawkers. Any of your husband's work friends can call you and arrange to see you separately in a neutral environment like a diner to offer their condolences, if they wish.

If the company had a SEP pension plan-- Simplified Employee Pension--your husband could well still be eligible to receive a current year's company contribution so long as he was considered an "eligible employee" at the time of his death. He does NOT have to be an employee as of the last-day-of-the-year in order to be eligible for that year's contribution.

If your husband was the business owner or a partner in the company where he worked, you will request your face-to-face meeting with the remaining company officers and your Certified Public Accountant, as there will be myriad areas to explore with regard to benefits owed you. You will be determining whether a buy-sell agreement was in place, and if so, was it funded with a life insurance policy, and/or what pension plans are in existence and what is your husband's vested interest, for starters.

Active Duty Servicemen Benefits

Active duty servicemen's widows are the most obvious class of widows who typically are notified of their husband's death by their employer, the US Government. While the person who called/visited you may have given you contact information, I've listed a couple of sources on the Internet for your information.

For active duty servicemen widow benefits related to Survivor Benefit Plan insurance, see this site:

www.military.com/benefits/survivor-benefits/the-survivor-benefit-plan-explained.html.

For information on Military Funeral & Burial Arrangements, Death Gratuity, Disbursement of Pay and Allowances, Dependency and Indemnity Compensation, Surviving Family Benefits, Ongoing Military Benefits, and a Survivor's Resource List, please visit:

www.militaryonesource.mil/12038/Project %20Documents/MilitaryHOMEFRONT/Casu alty%20Assistance/Survivors%20Guide.pdf.

For compassionate care for all survivors of a deceased military service person, call TAPS, Tragedy Assistance Program for Survivors, at 1-800-959-TAPS (8277) or visit www.TAPS.org.

Social Security

Phone Social Security (SS) at 1-800-772-1213 or log onto the Internet at www.socialsecurity.gov to inform them of your husband's death. Ask them what documents you will need to gather and bring to your face-to-face appointment. If you had been married, divorced or widowed before ask what you will need to bring related to those marriages/divorces so you have all the documents you need.

This is an information gathering meeting only. You will receive the information on any and all benefits you may be eligible to receive, both now and in the future. DO NOT MAKE A DECISION at this meeting!

I cannot stress enough that making the proper Social Security benefits decision can be very complicated. In order not to potentially sacrifice literally groups of zeros, consult a fee-only CFP® for a Social Security maximization analysis. Chapter 15 details various SS benefits.

While I have mentioned health insurance, Medigap insurance, life insurance and long-term care insurance here, rest assured you will cover the particulars of each of these in your meeting with your fee-only CFP® (covered in the next chapter).

Credit Card Companies

Phone each credit card company where your husband had credit cards, including those companies where both of your names were listed on the account. (The phone number is on the back of each card.)

Immediately ask to speak with a supervisor as you don't want to waste time with an underling service representative. Tell the supervisor that your husband died and ask them how to transfer his credit line, or that of your joint credit line, over into your singular name.

You will be responsible for repayment of any debt accrued on any credit cards with both of your names, yet whether you are responsible to pay off debt on cards in his singular name is highly debatable.

I've heard of instances where an attorney's call to the credit card company can result in the absolution of these debts, or at least reduction of them, particularly in instances where you, the survivor, were ignorant of these cards and/or debt balances.

If you are indeed found responsible for the repayment of debts in his singular name, request a payment plan that can work with your budget. Additionally, ask the supervisor for a reduced interest rate, given your circumstances. These supervisors are human, so relay your story to them in a calm manner that you are prepared to honor the obligation of repayment. Yet without his salary you are significantly stretched financially, so is it possible that you can receive a lesser percentage interest rate?

I advise that you emphatically state that while you lost your husband, you do NOT want to lose your good credit rating; you are conscious about not being late with payments that would otherwise erode your existing credit score. (The credit card company doesn't want to write off the debt, so many will work with you, if you speak with the right representative.) If the supervisor you speak with is unhelpful or unsympathetic with changing your terms so that you can repay the debt(s), ask for that person's supervisor until you get a person who will work with you. You deserve courtesy and excellent service, yes you do.

Write down every name of every representative you speak with, along with the date and time you spoke with them. This comes in very handy when you need to speak with another supervisor. You can say, "When I spoke with Susan Jones, a customer service supervisor on Thursday, September 2nd, at 4:15pm she said she was sending me new paperwork with the repayment plan we discussed."

This practice is very helpful in every facet of your life; it tends to separate out the people serious about getting answers from the whiners. Yes, you are grieving, yet you also need and expect answers and considerations, and I pray you get both. (Your fee-only CERTIFIED FINANCIAL PLANNER™ could be a terrific help in these matters by arranging 3-way telephone conference calls with you and the credit card supervisor, taking the lead role in these types of negotiations…just sayin'.)

Summary Takeaway:

Everyone doesn't have to be notified and met with immediately. Between the immediate demands and everything else, you need time to feel, breathe, emote, and breathe some more. And you deserve everything written down so you can read and re-read the material, noting your questions on each page.

Chapter 12
Why a Fee-Only CFP® is Essential

My dear late friend Dr. Susan Jeffers wrote many landmark best-selling books. *Feel the Fear and Do It Anyway* is principal among them. Susan said, "If everybody feels fear when approaching something totally new in life, yet so many are out there 'doing it' despite the fear, then we must conclude that fear is not the problem...rather how we HOLD the fear."

She created what she coined the Pain-Power Continuum to inform us that it's not the fear itself that is daunting to each of us. She adds, "The secret in handling fear is to move yourself from a position of pain to a position of power."

Her continuum is anchored with the words Power and Pain at opposite ends. She explains that the emotions that are evoked when we hold our fear from a position of Pain are Helplessness, Depression and Paralysis. Conversely, the emotions evoked when we hold our fear from a position of Power are Choice, Excitement and Action.

The empowering aspect of this continuum is that we are free to move from Pain to Power; we have a choice that we can exercise as we wish. Knowing that we can act to empower ourselves, we are not as trapped in our pain.

It's How We HOLD Our Fear
Dr. Susan Jeffers' Continuum

PAIN--------------------------------**POWER**
Helplessness.........................…...Choice
Depression.......................…..Excitement
Paralysis................................….......Action

Feel the Fear and Do It Anyway
Fawcett Columbine, NY, 1987 p. 34

Clearly, over our lifetimes, we've all experienced situations in which our fear(s) paralyzed us, yet other times when we were able to move through previously held fears. I find Dr. Jeffers' continuum image empowering as it illustrates that we can, and do, slide along such a scale; no current state of how we are holding our fear need be permanent. We can **decide** to inch a bit closer to holding that fear from a position of Power in order to assuage some of our Pain. Dr. Jeffers asserts we have a choice, always. I concur.

So, the first choice in entering your Financial Decision Zone is, who will be your financial planner? This person will serve as your navigational captain, a most vital role in better ensuring not only your financial success, but also your movement from pain to power.

I will speak interchangeably about financial planners as *she* and as *he* throughout the book with no particular preference to gender.

As you may know, anyone can hang out a shingle stating that he or she is a financial planner. And with unemployment at record levels, a number of people who have been laid off of their jobs have decided to try their hand at financial advising. Even some of the media's financial pundits often hold themselves out to be financial experts or financial planners. Sadly, there are no current regulations to prevent this.

So how do widows find and hire competent and ongoing excellent financial, legal and tax advisors? Thankfully, within the arena of financial planners, how the planner is paid actually serves as a valuable tool in helping you make that decision. Yes, it really is that simple. The three types of compensation amongst financial representatives, advisors and planners follow:

1. **Commissionable:** earn product commissions, period.
2. **Fee-based:** charge a fee on a written plan (which not so surprisingly often recommends the purchase of a life insurance or annuity product) PLUS earn commissions on products sold.
3. **Fee-only:** charge a fee for their advice, period. This fee is typically either a flat annual amount or it is based upon a

percentage of the assets they manage for you.

Fee-only financial planners avoid the direct conflict of interest that the other two pose. Fee-only financial planners operate under, and are professionally held to, a fiduciary oath of serving the client needs FIRST and foremost.

This is NO time for you to have to defend your rights as a consumer or be charged with the responsibility of determining whether a financial product is suitable for you or not. Although you may have to search a little, the search will prove worthwhile because of the high standards to which fee-only planners are held. **Seek out a fee-only CERTIFIED FINANCIAL PLANNER™ who will work with you towards the singular goal of helping you to achieve YOUR goals, period.**

If the financial planner does not immediately inform you about how they are paid, it's likely that he is paid by commissions. If their business card or stationery states, "Securities offered through…." they are commissioned salespeople, period, regardless of any and all bold claims of independence.

Commissioned salespeople and stockbrokers' training focuses on specific knowledge of the product(s) they sell. Granted, they have a keen understanding of the rates of **commission** paid on each product sold, and also whether or not there is a renewal, trail commission to be paid annually in future years.

Their business card typically identifies them as *agent* or *representative* of the companies whose products they sell, as do those of most fee-based financial planners. While commissionable and fee-based representatives are all forbidden from selling *unsuitable* products, their allegiance is to the companies they represent, not to you, the consumer.

In the case of commissioned life insurance salespeople, too many lack the training or experience of advising the client before the sale. They may also lack understanding of the potential adverse consequences if the application isn't completed correctly; i.e., if the correct ownership isn't specified, as you'll read about in Chapter 18, in LuAnn's sad scenario.

Naturally, it takes longer to do business correctly, often elongating the time that a commissionable salesperson or a fee-based representative has to wait to receive their commission. So they may be tempted to take shortcuts. Or they simply may not understand the correct way of doing business. While we can all empathize with a guy's or gal's right to earn a living, these shortcuts can and do carry grave consequences for consumers.

To repeat, I am NOT unequivocally bashing product salespeople here; I was one of them for the first 15 years of my career, before the fee-only financial planner option existed. However, I was one of an elite few who never sold anyone a financial product that I hadn't purchased for myself, nor did I represent or sell products to clients that were inappropriate, or in any way unsuitable. It's safe to say, I'm not confident that my standards were (or are) shared by the vast majority of the commissioned salesperson field.

I have since obtained years of education, training and experience that have equipped me to advise clients objectively on life-giving, complex financial matters.

If you want to avoid pain, potentially irreversible consequences (without significant costs), and additional expenses, **the LEAD professional on your financial team MUST be a fee-only CFP®.**

Statistics on the average fee-only CFP® follow:

• She is held to the **strictest fiduciary standard**, that of **serving the client's needs first and foremost**, unlike commission sales people, who serve their sponsoring company's needs and their own needs, generating several levels of commissions on product sales.

• He has completed course work and passed a rigorous competency exam on Income Tax, Investing, Legal, Insurance & Risk, Estate Planning, Cash Flow & Debt Management disciplines.

• She has practiced for, on average, over 15 years in the field of financial planning and investment advising as a CERTIFIED FINANCIAL PLANNER™.

- He has completed a minimum of 60 hours of continuing education every two years.

- She is equipped to produce periodic and systematic investment performance reports which clearly show you your portfolio's rate of return as well as the rates of return for your portfolio's *benchmark* (or comparative) averages, sometimes referred to as Indexes. (Neither stock brokers, commissionable sales people or fee-based advisors are equipped to provide ongoing, systematic investment performance reports, as do the fee-only CFPs®.)

When your lead professional fee-only CERTIFIED FINANCIAL PLANNER™ identifies a need for an insurance policy--life, disability, long-term care, homeowners, auto, liability--she can, and does, make specific recommendations for either the purchase of no-load insurance products where available, or the purchase of loaded products. In the latter case, she will refer you to commission salespeople whom she knows will represent excellent products as well as deliver great service. This commission salesperson then works hand-in-glove with the lead fee-only CFP® introducing the proper product for the need, and implementing the purchase or issuance. In this way she ensures the proper titling and/or ownership of the product. Finally, she arranges for the premium payment(s).

Regardless, this coordination of planning and product integration is KEY to a favorable financial plan's working smoothly, both initially and in the ensuing years. In the case of a referral to a commissioned sales person, that agent earns their full commission.

The fee-only CFP® is NOT paid any commissions, any over rides, or even a referral fee. His concern is simply that the correct product has been proposed and purchased to protect the insured's underlying risk. This is the proper role of a commissioned salesperson; i.e., to be brought in **after** the fee-only CFP® has objectively assessed your situation for potential "product gaps."

Financial professionals need to know what questions to ask a prospective client. Too many times I have asked basic questions of commissioned salespeople and they don't understand the question, let alone the answer, or even why I may be asking it. This is the scary consequence of their ignorance. There is an URGENT need for the public, and especially vulnerable widows, to understand about the various types of financial planners. How each type is paid correlates to what services and recommendations she is trained to provide.

I am beating this drum so loudly because it is my fervent mission to save you from serious financial harm. You may have guessed by now that I've seen groups of zeroes of widows' money wasted on paid commissions for unsuitable products.

I've heard too many sad tales of widows being promised that this particular financial advisor or financial representative would serve them on a **complimentary basis** during the first six months or one year. It sounded so innocent, yet a boatload of damage can happen in just one appointment or with one product sale by a commission only or fee-based representative.

It's too late to recover the commission you paid when you deal first with a product salesperson and later seek out the fee-only planner. It must occur in the reverse order to ensure you won't be irrevocably overcharged.

Because of the excellent pedigree of fee-only CFP®s in terms of years of experience, their fiduciary oath, and their stringent Continuing Education requirements--all resulting in only a relatively select number of such planners nationwide--I feel most confident in their ability to prepare a comprehensive written financial plan. That plan will include a Monte Carlo probability analysis to guide your investment decisions to best ensure you won't run out of money as you age, as well as accomplish the following:

• Tease out your short, medium and long-term goals, attaching approximate price tags to each.

• Identify what risks you need to pass on to an insurance company and what risks you will assume personally.

- Coordinate your (or those of your late husband's) group health, life, disability and long-term care benefits at work with those you may have purchased individually.

- Overview your property & casualty insurance for proper dwelling, contents as well as liability coverages--coordinating your auto and homeowners or renter's policies with that of your umbrella insurance policy.

- Review your last two years of income tax returns--federal and state, if applicable--for tax filing status as well as applicable deductions. You are permitted to file under Qualifying Widow status for 2 years after the year of your husband's death if you meet those standards.

- Prepare a balance sheet, ensuring that cash flow and debt management are optimized.

- Recommend appropriate college education savings plans, if necessary.

- Advise you 1) on the **best age** to apply, and 2) for which particular Social Security benefit(s) you should receive first.

- Review your legal agreements, including your will, power of attorney, child custody agreement, living will, medical directive, trust documents, and the like--to determine if they still provide the desired protection, direction and eventual distribution of your estate.

- Coordinate your current investments with ones that are, in that planner's expertise, not only suitable, yet most likely able to meet your goals, all within your risk tolerance.

You will agree on the frequency of regular meetings with your fee-only CFP®, which will occur either in person or via telephone, Skype, or webinar screen-sharing sessions on the computer, so that you feel comfortable with the process, are updated on the performance of your plan, and are advised of any new recommendations.

At least annually, your investments will be rebalanced back to the original asset allocation, to maintain the agreed-upon risk exposure. You agree to update the planner as to any material changes in your personal and professional circumstances so that the changes can be melded into the plan recommendations and/or strategies.

It is because of my degree of confidence in fee-only CFP®s that I do not delve further into specific recommendations of any particular investment discipline in this book, nor any other specific facet of the financial planning process. Rather, I choose to trust their comprehensive process and corresponding advice, given their command of the facts, your individual circumstances, and the trusting relationship you will undoubtedly build over time.

Regardless of your net worth, you need a qualified fee-only CFP® who will take a fiduciary responsibility for the overall sea worthiness of your financial plan and the various financial products you will own. This ensures that everything is poised to work exactly how it needs to work, precisely when it's called upon to work. In this way your investments will provide however much money you need, when you need it. It's certainly your money to do with as you please. Yet if it doesn't serve you when you need it, what was the point of saving during all those years?

How valuable is a good night's sleep right about now? One of my clients told me, "After our first appointment I enjoyed my first full night's sleep since Roger died six months ago."

I believe you, too, will want that level of expertise at your side, a qualified professional who "has your back." It's your right; exercise it. You are worth it; you deserve every happiness. Time and health are your two most valuable assets. Protect both.

Imagine the relief of relying upon your financial planner to telephone conference you onto the phone line with each of the aforenamed parties. Not only does it take the weight off of you to initiate each call, she can also prompt you to ask whatever questions you may temporarily forget.

Here are two great resources for locating a qualified fee-only CFP®: www.napfa.org and www.garrettplanningnetwork.com.

I recommend that you interview at least two such planners, perhaps asking them to complete a form that I feel is informative to learn about their approach. This form is available on both of my websites www.DebraLMorrison.com and www.EmpoweredRetirement.com or by calling 973-709-2244. This completed form will help to identify which one professional you may feel more comfortable communicating with. Most certainly, this is a relationship-built business.

If you don't see a fee-only CFP® in your geographic area, call and interview at least two planners who practice near one of your children or your best friend(s), so if you would be traveling to visit them, you could also see your financial planner as well. Or consider doing business remotely; it's far easier these days with email and computer screen sharing via the Internet, or Skype. While I could never service even a modicum of the number of widows reading this book, I personally have clients in 13 states and can attest to the ease of any fee-only CFP® doing business remotely.

Summary Takeaway:

To reduce the possibility of a negative outcome or series of outcomes, which could very well cost you tens if not hundreds of thousands of dollars, choose wisely who will head your financial team, and choose only a fee-only CFP®.

Chapter 13
Organizing Your Finances

If you are like most widows--heck, most women--I know, much of your pain and ensuing angst is around the fact that you don't know what you don't know about money.

As Dr. Susan Jeffers stated in *Feel the Fear and Do It Anyway*, if we are alive, we will encounter fears, period. We will commit, however, to moving through our fears, taking small baby steps forward into our own personal power.

We're human; we make mistakes. Your beloved made mistakes! We may not have known about all of them, yet rest assured, he made mistakes over the years. But I would be surprised if those mistakes unraveled your entire financial health.

Organizing our financial information is a great first step towards better understanding what we don't know. Give yourself permission to take the information gathering slowly at first; acclimating to both the change that was thrust upon you and the positive new change you are creating.

As you move through stages of accepting the fact that your husband is indeed gone, the next steps will be easier. I say that because I've witnessed countless widows being more able to move forward once they accept that their role has indeed changed. These widows are no less sad, mind you; yet they now claim their responsibility to move forward and they begin strategizing and taking action steps accordingly.

Even if you did handle certain aspects of your finances while your husband was alive, most likely you did so with either a subconscious or conscious awareness that you could always ask him questions, or lean on his judgment.

Maybe you didn't even think about it much; as you encountered a financial issue or problem, you'd both put your heads together and solve it. The weight of not having your mate to discuss your financial decisions with now is heavy; so instead of carrying on in your normal, competent manner, you question how on earth you used to do it. Sound familiar?

We've made great progress on these first few steps which are to feel, grieve, pick up your emotional pieces, make immediate notifications, honor the 6-month no-decision zone, and begin to unwind your emotions from your money, writing down your emotions and all those money messages--negative and positive--so that we can consciously deal with them.

We'll now start with whatever your situation--whether you had time to review the location of important documents with your husband or you didn't. I well understand that even if your husband's death followed a term of sickness, he may not have been in a position, or mood, to discuss finances. Money conversations are often difficult for couples, especially if he feared he didn't prepare well, or leave you *enough* money. Please forgive yourself for perhaps not bringing up money matters amidst your caregiving and the precious time you shared. It is okay; either way, it's okay.

Regardless, this may be a task that you want to call a friend in to help you with, because it often evokes strong emotions. Sit quietly and reflect on which friend or family member is most supportive of you now and call them for help.

By now you have an idea of what time of the day your thoughts are clearer than others. I realize that now, everything is relative, yet are you more of an early morning or late night person? This may well have changed since your husband's death, yet what time of the day has been, on average, productive for you lately? Start this organizational process during that time of day and aim to get at least one thing done each day so you can feel accomplished and that you are making progress.

I advise that you go ahead and open up any and every possible drawer, your safety deposit box, cabinets and whatnot to eventually pull out every financial piece of paper that exists.

Open All Unopened Mail
Open all the financial mail that may be sitting unopened, including yet not limited to:

- bank statements,
- brokerage statements,
- group insurance statements,
- company pension plans,
- 401(k)s or 403(b)s.

These days a lot of information is kept on the computer, so hopefully your husband left a list of passwords. (Allow me to make a clarion call here for **you** to remember to write down your passwords on your calendar or a piece of paper that you put in your safety deposit box or somewhere where your eventual heirs can find it, because it will make your eventual estate settlement proceedings a whole lot easier).

If you say, "Well, I change my password a lot," pick a password that you like (perhaps the name of your family's favorite pet Skippy) and put the number one behind it. When you're required to update it (as most sites require), put the next successive number after that same password, and instantly record that update also on your paper calendar.

Hopefully upon your death, a thinking survivor will look at your last calendar password entry and enter that exact password, or perhaps add a successive number to the last one recorded in order to access your records. In this way, your survivors will be further ahead, knowing that your password most likely begins with Skippy, followed by a number, rather than having absolutely no idea of where to start.

Alternatively, you may search Google for an Internet password management program, like www.LastPass.com to help with this task.

Make a Series of Piles

Okay, back to our organization project. In the beginning, I recommend you make a series of piles. Keep bills separate from bank account statements, brokerage account statements, and anything else that has numbers all over it.

Bills First!

We'll address the bills first. Some of your bills may be paid automatically from a credit card, or your checking account, or your investment brokerage account. (A brokerage account is an account that is capable of holding many different types of investments--mutual funds, stocks, bonds, certificates of deposits, and even limited partnerships. The name on the top of the statement identifies who the custodian of these accounts is; in other words, who is holding this combination of investments). Some familiar custodians are TD Ameritrade, Schwab, Fidelity, etc.

The best way of finding out whether bills are paid automatically out of any of your accounts is to either look at the vendor's statements that come in the US "snail mail," or in your email, or your late partner's email account, or your credit card, or your checking or brokerage account statements.

On the electric bill, for example, it will clearly state somewhere near the "amount owed" box that an automatic payment has been made, or is scheduled to be made. On the credit card statement, it will clearly state in the list of monthly charges, ABC Electric and the amount paid. So, you can simply cross reference these two statements for this information.

Make sure that all of the bills that you know about are paid for this month. If you missed a bill for any reason and are either called, or mailed, a notification of a pending late charge, simply respond to the vendor, explain the situation, and work with them for a swift solution. Ask each vendor if they will accept payment for their bill via a credit card and if so, set that up, utilizing one specific (lower interest) credit card for routine bills. For now, choose the credit card offering the most attractive travel reward program--one that credits you with either valuable frequent flier miles, or points, depending upon your card's promotional offerings. In addition to accruing future travel benefits, it will also serve to automate your bill paying, so you are NEVER late at any time in the future.

Being late in your bill paying will significantly reduce your credit score. So aim to pay each and every bill on time, starting this very month!

Credit Scores & Reports

Surprisingly all your financial activity gets recorded on your credit report. Your credit score will determine what interest rate you pay on future loans or lines of credit, which will, in turn, translate into either a bigger or smaller monthly payment on your next car loan or mortgage.

Your credit score is amazingly important, so log onto www.myfico.com to learn more about what factors carry more weight on attaining or maintaining a great credit score.

A poor credit score will cost you a lot more money the next time you wish to qualify for a mortgage, enter an assisted living facility, buy a car, rent an apartment, or apply for a job. People infer a ton of information from your credit score and base your borrowing rate on how good your score is. The better your score, the lower interest rate you'll be charged. So best to work on improving your credit score right now. With a great credit score you could easily save yourself upwards of $100 per month on a new car loan or several hundred dollars a month in mortgage payments.

There are three Credit Reporting Agencies-- TransUnion, Experian and Equifax--each giving you a slightly different score. Various lenders will access any number of these, if not all of these, so it's important to know your score with each agency.

While these reports generally cost money, you are able to obtain one free credit report--

one from each of the three major bureaus--
every twelve months. To do so, you can either
call 1-877-322-8228 or log onto the Internet
and type www.annualcreditreport.com in the
URL space at the top. Please simply type that
into your browser bar directly rather than doing
an Internet search, because otherwise you will
get all sorts of copycat sites that charge fees.

www.AnnualCreditReport.com is the single
best site where you can get your free annual
credit reports. These credit reports will also
serve as a handy cross reference to identifying
all your existing and closed accounts, as well as
those of your late husband if you held joint
accounts.

You will most likely find an error or two on
these reports, yet those can and should be fixed
quite easily by contacting the particular
company that has listed the erroneous
information to report the problem. They are
required to fix the error within 90 days, so your
credit score will improve accordingly.

Identity Theft Protection

To better protect yourself against Identity
Theft, do check your credit report now, using
only the above link:
www.AnnualCreditReport.com and then mark
on your calendar for exactly one year from
today, and two years from today, etc. when you
are eligible for another free credit check. Write
this URL address right onto your calendar--
whether you keep your records online, or on a

paper calendar. You don't want to be fumbling around in a year or two for the proper address.

Identity theft abounds, and sadly some cyber criminals target the deceased and their survivors, so take action on this now, as having to regain your good name and credit after identity theft takes valuable time and energy!

For further protection change your passwords if you use ones similar to that of your late husband. Avoid opening up suspicious emails that appear in your inbox. While spam folders catch some of the "junk" mail that each of us receives on a daily basis, too much still slips through, many of which have enticing subject lines to lure us into opening them. Please resist this temptation if you don't recognize the sender's email address!

You may wish to sign up for an identity theft service where the provider charges anywhere from $9.95 to $29.95 each month in exchange for sending you any changes to your credit report, for example. This can add to your piece of mind, and I do recommend that you obtain such a service, at least for this next year. It's a small price to pay to relieve your fear that someone may be illegally using your credit cards or bank accounts (or those of your husband) to make fraudulent purchases. Most of your credit card companies offer this type of protection, as well as www.myfico.com and www.lifelock.com.

If you are a victim of identity theft, immediately report it to your local police department as well as the US Post Office. Send the police report to all your creditors and credit-reporting agencies. Additionally, complete the form on this site: www.consumer.ftc.gov.

If you are receiving a lot of "junk" email in your inbox you can and should right click on each one, and select "block sender" or some such language. Also, you can adjust the spam settings on your Internet browser.

On my current version of Firefox, at the very top of the screen, left click on Tools, then left click on Options, then left click on Security, and follow the directions. My apologies if Firefox changes this in future releases, yet this will give you at least a cursory idea of how to accomplish this. Alternatively, call in most 6 or 8 year old kids and they can do it for you--in exchange for a brownie, or chocolate-chip cookie, of course.

Federal Income Tax Return

Locate your latest year's Federal and State Income Tax returns (if you live in a state that levies State Income Tax). If you are unable to find your income tax returns, not to worry. As you gain access to the Internet, just go to this address to receive a copy of your return:

www.irs.gov/uac/Newsroom/How-to-Get-a-Transcript-or-Copy-of-a-Prior-Year-Tax-Return

If you only need a transcript, which shows your tax information line by line, as well as the detail of your wages and income information, I invite you to visit this link for your tax transcript:

www.irs.gov/Individuals/Get-Transcript

Each of these websites offers to email you the information or mail the information via the United States Postal Service, otherwise referred to in this book as *snail mail*. I strongly recommend that you choose the latter. This is FAR too much information to send through email, regardless of the security claims listed.

Schedule B of your Federal Tax Return is divided into Part 1 (Interest) and Part II (Ordinary Dividends). This Schedule B lists all your itemized investments and the corresponding amounts of earnings on these investments on which you paid income taxes last year. See how this can also serve as a cross-reference tool in locating more of your assets? In other words, if you see an entry of ABC Brokerage Account on the left side, marked Payer, and $3,000 on the right side under Amount, it tells you that you earned $3,000 last year on the investment in ABC Brokerage account. (One could reasonably deduce then, if one estimated earning 2% annually, that particular investment might be worth some $150,000, which is calculated by dividing $3,000 by .02).

Your Federal Income Tax return can be a treasure-trove of information if you know where to look. Often W-2 forms are stapled to your tax return. They too provide clues as to additional benefits your husband was paying for. Review your Federal Income Tax return and note questions to ask your CPA.

Please note that IF you have a dependent child you may be permitted (if you meet the standards) to file as *Qualifying Widow* for two years after the date of your husband's death, for Federal Income Tax purposes. (You are able to file *Married Filing Jointly* in the year of his death, if you choose.) Ask your CPA to run your taxes using each filing status to determine which one saves you more money. Additionally, either status--*Married Filing Jointly* or *Qualifying Widow* (if you qualify)--may result in fewer taxes than you would owe in future years filing as a *Single Taxpayer* (unless you would remarry). So strategies such as converting a Traditional IRA to a Roth IRA, or receiving extra income, may well be more attractive in these next two years.

Some widows choose to set up a foundation or charitable account in the name of their husband, yet the tax deductions resulting from either may be worth far more in a year in which you file with *Single Taxpayer* status. Or you dovetail both--receiving extra income in the year you set up the charitable entity, so one taxable event is otherwise offset with a tax-deductible event.

Current Year's Receipts

Designate a large box or two that will serve as a place to store any current year receipts for expenses or bills that you pay. The reason you will keep those is that some of them may have an impact on your income tax return. You will determine later whether these expenses can be deducted from your income in computing how much income tax you will owe this, and next, year. For now, just put the receipts for everything you spend money on, into this box.

Identify Piles

Now to those piles! You've sorted first by the title on the top of each statement. So, for example, you put all the ABC Bank statements in one pile, and all the XYZ mutual fund statements in another pile.

Next, highlight both the account number, the account holder's name, and the date on each statement, so that this information is easily identifiable whenever you look at it. It will help to be able to quickly recite this highlighted pertinent information if you need to answer a question on the telephone with a service person. HINT: Two of the very first questions asked are, "What account number are you inquiring about?" and "Under what name is the account registered?"

If you find that you have two or more different account numbers with the ABC bank, for example, make a second (& subsequent, if applicable) ABC Bank statement pile(s)--one pile for each account number. You get the picture.

Third, highlight the total amount of the investment on each and every statement, along with the date of that particular statement.

Slowly but surely, as you keep at it, one piece of paper at a time, you will begin to feel pumped about bringing order to your finances, or perhaps to what had seemed to be financial chaos. What once appeared like an insurmountable sea of unopened envelopes, complete with the accompanying fear of what might be inside, has now been tamed. Each statement with tons of numbers printed on each page, DOES in fact, tells its own story, once we learn what we're looking for.

By now you have a cursory idea of how many different accounts your husband had, so you will note on a piece of notebook paper how many different accounts you have. I would not recommend amassing this information on your smart phone or computer just now. It's highly confidential, so I advise keeping this on a paper pad.

While an original death certificate is typically needed to change the registration on each account, sometimes a copy will suffice. You'll determine that answer as you meet, or speak, with your CFP® so as to limit your expense in purchasing originals from the funeral director. (Be sure to get some death certificates stating the cause of death.) You can always go back to the funeral director with a request for more, should you need them.

Summarize & Log Your Findings

Manually write down each account--the assets on one page, and the bills on another page, just to keep them separated. Record the account number, the registered name in which the account is titled, the current account balance, and in the case of the bills, whether a payment is due or not. If a payment is due, such as on a credit card, highlight the minimum amount and list that on your notepad along with the due date.

If interest is being charged on a loan or a credit card balance, write down the loan interest percentage that is printed on the statement. Keep an eye out for high interest rates on loans you may be paying, and highlight those interest rates in yet another color. Trust me; it will behoove you to address lowering those higher rates or paying those balances first so that you can pocket the monthly savings.

These organizational steps can feel like a huge assignment, and indeed they are! As I see it, however, you can either be daunted by it, or you can turn it into a game in order to get it done. You know my choice, of course.

Just as in the old television game called Concentration, you are really matching up your statements to the piles with other similar statements in it. Then you highlight the salient information on each statement, order that pile in chronological order (with the most current information on the top of the pile) and record the most current information on your paper pad. Now you may wish to 3-hole punch each statement and piece of related paper and file them under separate company or account tabs in 3-ring binders. *Voila!*

I suspect that completing this exercise will bring you HUGE relief. Essentially you've created a map of your financial landscape.

While you will surely lean on professional help along the way, YOU have demonstrated that you are the able groundskeeper. This is just simple executive organization, plain old common sense. And unlike feelings, it's all there in black and white. Things are different now; yes. Yet, you CAN do what needs doing. You ARE doing it. Congratulations!

Assets & Debt Tracking

I've partially completed two sample tracking sheets, to give you an example of what your asset and debt tracking sheets might look like when you complete this process.

First you will see the asset tracking sheet which I partially completed to serve as an example. The following page is the same sheet without any pre-filling of hypothetical data so you can enter your own details easily.

Second you will see a debt tracking sheet, again partially completed to serve as an example. That is followed by the same sheet without any pre-filling so you can enter your information. Feel free to visit my website: www.DebraLMorrison.com to down-load additional spreadsheets as you need them.

Example of Wise Widowed Woman's Asset Tracking Sheet

Institutional Account	Investment Type	Current Balance	IRA/ Taxable Nontaxable	Monthly Income	Registration Name	Phone # Contact	Call Details With Whom I Spoke	Result
ABC Bank 12345567	Certificate of Deposit (CD)	$10,000	Taxable	$17.00	Joint	800-232-2424	1/2/15 - Mr. Smith requested papers to change registration to my name	1/5/15 - Received papers signed & returned
ABC Mutual Fund 987654	Mutual Fund	$34,000	IRA	$55.00	My Name	877-242-3535	1/13/15 - Ms. Simple requested dividends to be reinvested	1/16/15 - Received email dividends now reinvested
QRS Mutual Fund 1788711	Mutual Fund	$57,000	Taxable	$95.00	Husband's Name	800-444-5000	1/2/15 - Ms. Smith requested my name on account	1/9/15 - Fee-Only Planner handled name change
XYZ Insurance Co. 95959S9	Life Insurance Proceeds	$300,000	Nontaxable		Husband's Name	866-543-9876	1/2/15 - Mr. Helpful called - offered to pay me 2% interest rate until I decide how to take the proceeds	1/5/15 - Called Fee-Only Financial Planner to discuss

Wise Widowed Woman's Asset Tracking Sheet

Institutional Account	Investment Type	Current Balance	IRA/ Taxable Nontaxable	Monthly Income	Registration Name	Phone # Contact	Call Details With Whom I Spoke	Result

Example of Wise Widowed Woman's Debt Tracking Sheet

Company & Account #	Account Type	Outstanding Balance	Total Line $	Current Interest Rate	Minimum Payment Due	Paid Last Month	Interest Rate Details	Phone Number Details	Call Details With Whom I Spoke	Result
ABC Bank 12345678910	Visa	$3,400	5,000	12.99%	$85.00	$85.00	18.99% cash advance rate	800-232-2424	1/2/15 - Mrs Prim, supervisor, Austin TX - requested line increase	1/5/15 - Credit Line increase to 10k
Super Bank 88465725679	Master Card	$9,400	10,400	0% teaser rate	$39.56	$39.56	12.99% after 12/15	877-242-3535	Note to self Mark on calendar to payoff before December, 2015	
LMB Bank 17388711	Mortgage	$193,000	N/A	4.25%	$949.44	$949.44	Fixed for 12 years	866-987-6544	1/12/15 - Mr. Worel. Asked for auto mortgage payment via checking	1/13/15 - Received auto checking notice from local bank
XYZ Credit Union 95959S9	Car Loan	$7,400	N/A	4%	$218.48	$218.48	none	800-123-4567	1/13/15 - Mrs. Adam. Asked for payoff figure	1/14/15 - Called Fee-Only Financial Planner to discuss

Wise Widowed Woman's Debt Tracking Sheet

Company & Account #	Account Type	Outstanding Balance	Total Line $	Current Interest Rate	Minimum Payment Due	Paid Last Month	Interest Rate Details	Phone Number Details	Call Details With Whom I Spoke	Result

Summary Takeaway:

The best way to combat fear is with facts and taking action! We will be fact gatherers...and in that process we will be fear busters, moving from pain to power on Dr. Susan Jeffers' continuum, depicted in Chapter 12.

Chapter 14
Surprises

Unfortunately in too many instances, the discovery process of emptying drawers and files and reading US snail mail and emails, may result in the uncovering of any number of your husband's secrets. You may find that he:

- had a secret Post Office box address,

- had another lover,

- financially supported another lover,

- had extra credit cards that are maxed out,

- had extra lines of credit--secured or unsecured--that he maxed out,

- had money in foreign savings or checking accounts,

- had falsified your jointly filed income tax returns,

- had failed to pay bills, perhaps for months,

- had made poor investments,

- had an expensive addiction, and/or

- had failed to pay the life insurance premiums, or actively cancelled the policy.

Both the secrecy of these events and now your discovery of them will surely result in any combination of feelings including but not limited to infuriation, a sense of being humiliated, shamed, crushed, or wounded, or profound sadness. I am deeply sorry for this additional pain and I advise you to immediately call a clinical licensed psychologist to set up an appointment to help process this additional grief.

My dear friend, Dr. Marj Steinfeld, has 27 years' experience in private practice psychotherapy in Pompton Lakes, New Jersey, and reports a marked increase in this phenomenon. In the last year alone she has counseled three widows through the ordeal of processing these secrets!

These betrayals of one severity or another add yet another layer of complexity to the grieving process. It will be absolutely necessary to forge through these feelings before taking any tangible steps forward. You must ensure that your reactions are not self-sabotaging.

The additional sorrow of discovering any of these (or other) indiscretions is that you may feel so entirely mortified that you feel you can't divulge this information even to a trusted psychologist. I beg of you, please dismiss that feeling right now. This is information that is FAR too heavy for you to manage without professional help.

Most likely if you have discovered surprises, your husband may have suffered from an addiction that felt too overwhelming or embarrassing for him to admit, so that's why he did what he did. Yet that's past now. You are in the present, and have to process all this information while awash in a whirlpool of emotions. Rest assured, clinical licensed psychologists have ample experience dealing with all of this. If necessary, you may choose to seek prescription medication from a licensed psychiatrist, which may hasten the recovery process.

You can heal from any number of these surprises with the proper support and advice, and I am confident that addressing them sooner rather than later is best. If the surprises involve finances, there are particular routes that can be taken to straighten out your credit rating, etc., so that you can move forward.

Alternatively, declaring bankruptcy could provide a new beginning. While that may sound either extreme or daunting IF that turns out to be the best alternative for you to rebuild your financial base for a profitable future, you and your fee-only CFP® can manage it.

Please do remember the Serenity Prayer:

GOD grant me the Serenity to accept the things I cannot change, the Courage to change the things I can, and Wisdom to know the difference.

Summary Takeaway:

If in your discovery process of sorting through mail and files, you discover unpleasant surprises, get immediate psychological help. If you find none of these adverse surprises you may wish to stop right now and say a heartfelt Thank You prayer!

Chapter 15
Potential Income Sources

Ok, now you have amassed your separate piles, which probably signify a good part of your finances. Additional potential income sources follow--some or all of which you can explore.

Social Security Survivor with Young Children Benefit

If you are supporting a child who is under age 16 and your late husband worked and contributed to Social Security or the Railroad Retirement Benefits for at least 10 years, you are eligible to receive a monthly Survivor's Benefit up until your youngest child attains age 16.

Currently you will receive 75% of your husband's Full Retirement Age Social Security benefit as a widow caring for an under age 16 child of a worker, subject to the Family Benefit maximum limits.

Social Security Widow's Survivor Benefit

A widow's benefit CAN equal 100% of her husband's PIA (Primary Insurance Amount) **if** she waits until her FRA (Full Retirement Age) to collect. (Note: if, however your husband began receiving benefits at his age 62, the most you will receive is the widow's limit provision of 81.5% of his PIA, if you apply at your FRA.)

The *earliest* you can claim a Social Security Survivor Benefit is age 60, or age 50 if you are disabled. Depending upon your age, you may experience what are commonly referred to as "gap years," where no Social Security Survivor's benefits are payable; i.e., the years between your youngest child's reaching age 16 and your turning age 60. You and your CFP® will plan how your other assets can supply your needed income for these "gap years."

Electing to receive Social Security Survivor Benefits at your age 60 will 1) subject you to the earnings test, and 2) result in a significantly REDUCED BENEFIT--you'll only receive 71.5% of your FRA (Full Retirement Age) Survivor's Benefit which would also result in lower lifetime cost of living raises. Waiting until age 62 or 65 gives you 81% or 95.3% respectively of your FRA benefit.

Realize that if you lose current Social Security benefits due to the earnings test because you are working, you MAY be credited with some of these forfeited benefits at a later time, depending on how you file; no guarantees.

If you have paid into Social Security such that you are eligible to receive your own Social Security Retirement Benefit, (and that benefit is **larger** than your survivor's benefit) you MAY file a *restricted application*, begin receiving a reduced 71.5% Survivor's Benefit at age 60, and then at any future age switch to begin receiving your own Social Security Retirement Benefit. If you are able to wait until your age 70 to switch from the Survivor Benefit to your own Retirement Benefit, you will accrue 8% delayed credits annually between your Full Retirement Age and age 70, significantly increasing your monthly check.

Alternatively if you've paid into Social Security, yet your own benefit is **smaller** than your Survivor Benefit, consider receiving your own Retirement Benefit at age 62 and defer receiving your Survivor Benefit until your FRA. (The agent at Social Security MAY inform you that you could be eligible to receive a higher current monthly Survivor Benefit, yet you will explain that you are choosing to delay the receipt of your Survivor Benefit, so that it won't be reduced.)

However, if your husband began receipt of his Social Security Retirement Benefit before his FRA, it may not pay you to wait until your FRA due to something called the RIB-LIM. The latter is **far too complicated** to address here; consult your CFP® to determine how best to maximize your benefits.

Social Security Children's Benefit

Unmarried children up to age 19 (who are full-time students in a secondary school) of a deceased parent are eligible to receive a monthly Children's Benefit. (See different rules for benefits paid to disabled adult children of a deceased parent). In either case, the Child's Benefit is equal to 75% of the widow's Full Retirement Age Survivor Retirement Benefit. Benefits to family members are limited to the family maximum--between 150%-180% of your husband's primary insurance amount.

Social Security General & Filing Info

Please note that Social Security agents are forbidden, not to mention unqualified, to render advice. They can dispense numbers, yes. They cannot advise, period.

That said and understood, Social Security's phone number is 800-772-1213, to obtain figures and/or arrange your telephone or in-office appointment. Social Security's website is: www.socialsecurity.gov. Their calculators are informative and I invite you to spend some time there for your own education.

What's your widow's FRA? Click here (http://www.ssa.gov/survivorplan/survivorcha rtred.htm) for the table with all the details.

In order to file to begin receiving a Social Security Survivor's Benefit you will need:

- SS numbers and birth certificates--your husband's, yours, any previous husband(s) and those of all dependent children,

- Yours and your late husband's two most recent W-2 forms or 1099 Forms (these are the forms stating annual gross and net earnings issued by his employer at the end of January, which are used to file Income Tax returns),

- Your late husband's death certificate- obtained from the funeral director, and

- Your marriage and/or divorce and/or previous husband's death certificate(s).

If your late husband was a United States Veteran, I advise that you Google "State Departments of Veterans Services" and select your state's web address for information on how to inform them of his passing. They will advise and counsel you as to what benefits may be available to you, both now and in the future.

As you speak with each individual--and I always immediately ask for a supervisor because I hate to waste time--note the first and last name of the individual with whom you are speaking, and the date and time of the call. This information is handy if you need to call back to follow up on a conversation. Should you be given incorrect information, having the time of day of your conversation would allow a supervisor to quickly locate, and listen to, your conversation on their recorded lines.

Here is contact info for the federal Veterans Affairs' offices, for your added reading. Yet your state office will serve as your advocate to navigate the federal benefits, and will be the best place for you to start.

- US Department of Veterans Affairs' phone is: 1-800-827-1000.

- US Department of Veterans Affairs' website is: www.va.gov.

Associations

If your late husband was a member of any associations, check what benefits may be available to you both now and in the future. Associations might include the following:

- American Automobile Association, www.aaa.com,

- American Association of Retired Persons, AARP, www.aarp.org,

- Masonic Lodge, geographically specific, so search the Internet for the closest Lodge location, and/or,

- Religious Orders, geographically specific, so search the Internet for the closest Order. There MAY be survivor's benefits available to you, as his survivor.

(If available, check your late husband's wallet for membership cards.)

Employer Provided Retirement Plan(s)

Your husband may have been covered by some type of company pension or retirement plan. He may have contributed his own money to the plan, which was most likely automatically deducted directly from his paycheck.

Perhaps he elected to **defer** a portion of his earnings into any number of various retirement plans, most commonly a Deferred Compensation Plan, or even a Profit Sharing Plan. The tax on this deferred compensation is deferred until the date(s) of withdrawal.

You can determine whether your late husband contributed to any pension plans by looking at his most recent W-2 statement. If the Retirement Plan in Box 13 is checked, he participated in a company Retirement Plan, most likely a 401(k), (or it would be called a 403(b) if he worked for a not-for-profit organization). Both the 401(k) and the 403(b) are pre-tax retirement plans; i.e., his taxable income was reduced dollar-for-dollar by the amount of his plan contributions.

Regardless of the type of plan, a Summary Plan Annual Statement lists the employee's share of the plan assets. If you cannot find this statement, it will most likely be included in the packet that his employer's Human Resources Department sends to you as a result of your notifying them, as covered earlier in this book.

If your late husband was a part or whole owner in a privately held company, contact your Certified Public Accountant for guidance on how to determine his share of the value of the company.

Refrain from signing off on paperwork or any documentation from ANY organization until you have had ample time to have this reviewed by one of your trusted professionals-- your attorney, your fee-only CFP®, and/or your

CPA, preferably a combination of these professionals.

Summary Takeaway:

Having ordered your finances, there may be other financial benefits due you from governmental agencies or your late husband's employer--whether he was still working or retired.

*The decisions of which Social Security benefit(s) to apply for, and when to begin receiving benefits, are FAR too complex to make without professional advice from a qualified fee-only CFP®. The lifetime payout amounts can vary **significantly**, upwards of tens if not hundreds of thousands of dollars in some cases, depending upon your age, your late husband's age, and both of your earnings. (Inform Social Security of any previous husbands you may have had, along with specifics of your divorce decree or his death certificate. You may well be eligible to receive benefits on his record as well.)*

Check out various websites of the organizations that your husband was a member of, or otherwise affiliated with, to determine if there may be any survivor benefits available.

If you didn't or couldn't order your finances, you could always consider hiring a temporary secretary or administrative assistant, the name of whom either your attorney or the funeral home director could supply.

Chapter 16
Missing or Inadequate Assets

What if assets are missing, or what if there's not enough money? Let's deal with both of these questions.

Missing Assets

What if after you sort through all the papers you have a strange sensation that there must be other assets that you haven't yet discovered? You feel quite sure that your husband had more money than this, or had at least one life insurance policy--the evidence of which is not showing up in your mail boxes or paper files.

I recommend that you log onto either www.unclaimed.com, www.unclaimedassets.com or www.missingassets.com. These are sites offering information on unclaimed property, missing money, veteran's benefits, matured US Savings Bonds, Credit Union Accounts...you name it.

Governmental assistance may be available, such as food stamps, or housing allowances, or free phones, for example. Section 8 housing accepts a portion of your income, for example. Check out these sites for up-to-date info:

- www.usgovinfo.about.com and
- www.ehow.com.

You may wish to search on Google, or any Internet search engine, for your particular state's websites for specific and timely information on assistance programs.

While your fee-only CFP® can partner with you to search in logical locations, you may wish to hire what's called a forensic accountant. A forensic accountant will do an exhaustive and investigative search for any and all of your husband's/decedent's missing assets. Yes, you would pay a fee (a portion of which may be income tax deductible, further reducing your cost) yet the fee may be small by comparison to either the findings of additional funds, or the peace of mind that comes from knowing you've indeed searched everywhere possible.

Inadequate Assets

Okay, let's talk about a different scenario than legitimate lost assets. Let's address the situation where you have found all the assets and the sources of income from your beloved, and you realize it is a very small amount, and not enough to see you through your old age. What to do?

Once you have your cash flows totaled, you will now delineate exactly what are your absolutely necessary expenses for survival. Everything else is subject to suspension right now. Often people can find ways to trim away hundreds of dollars each month, money that had been spent on items/experiences that can be suspended temporarily.

If you are able to work, you will probably begin interviewing for even a part-time job, or jobs, or a full-time job, based upon your skill set and how current your skills are to what the marketplace is seeking. Ask your friends if they know of any opportunities for a hard-working, committed, trustworthy individual, because you ARE that individual.

The job market landscape is changing such that you may land a job working from home if you have a computer and/or telephone. I invite you to think about what your friends value about you. Sometimes we undervalue our own gifts, experience and talents.

Realizing that folks are busy these days, it may surprise you what people are willing to pay big bucks for; things that you may simply do without thinking. Organizational skills or light book keeping skills could land you opportunities to help small businesses or new widows or busy single moms. Think in terms of what **value** you can bring to individuals and companies. And if that's also something you love to do, spread the word, build a website, print some business cards, and off you go, you entrepreneur you!

Alternatively you may need to seek refuge and save money by moving in with another family member or a friend for a finite period of time, a period which you both would negotiate ahead of time. At the end of that period, you may well renegotiate another period; yet everything would be agreed upon and written down to preserve boundaries--yours and theirs. This responsible approach should give both of you a comfort level and assurance that every measure is being taken to find an alternative solution. Having this arrangement or agreement in writing serves as a ready reminder for those days when you may need a boost to stay the course towards creating an inventive future.

Research meet-up groups in your neighborhood via www.meetup.com. Attending these meetings can be a ton of fun, and they don't cost much, if anything. So you're not breaking the bank to make some friends, and those friends might eventually lead to business opportunities.

Summary Takeaway:

Only you can answer your spending questions, and surprisingly, you will find both a temporary answer AND a more permanent, more pleasing answer by balancing your own budget. I have every confidence in your abilities and in your successes!

Part II

The Decision Zone is that space and time where we face choices that we've wisely put off until now. We have righted our ship and the sea of survival is calmer than when we were first capsized by that gigantic wave of grief. While we still grapple with huge unanswered questions, not the least of which is "WHY?" it's far more evident that however horrific our loss, it's indeed irreversible...and here we are. Accepting that fact is an important tipping point for us to better focus on creating our future, however unknown.

We now face the HOW choices. We cannot expect our scrambled minds to operate with complete and consistent acuity without the assistance of trusted navigational tools, timely strategies and qualified professionals on whom we can lean.

Chapter 17
Navigating the Decision Zone

Too often, widows don't know what they
don't know about finances. (I admit this is the
second time I'm making this statement). Not
only do they feel too intimidated to ask
questions, they are unsure of who they can trust
at such a vulnerable and uncertain time.

If this describes you, welcome: you're in the
right place. Hundreds of widows I've coached
report that my identifying and prioritizing
which decisions are important, and arming
them with tools, strategies and encouragement
to move on those decisions, has helped them
safely navigate the sea of uncertainty.

We'll identify and fill-in your information
gaps, so you, too, can make the wisest possible
decisions.

Additionally your **confidence** to make good
choices may well ebb and flow, yet I'll invite
you to remember some of your past successes
and take in all the sensory experiences of those
successes--how it felt, what it looked and
sounded like. The vivid remembrance of these
details and your great results will bolster your
confidence; after all, success breeds success.

Your   once-reliable-acuity-of-mind   may
occasionally falter. Yet instead of raising the

white flag, I will supply you with tools to regain your sea legs and competency in what you've managed before--balancing the checkbook, grocery shopping, child and pet care details, working outside the home and/or domestic engineering, in general--as well as venturing into uncharted waters in both your personal and financial lives. They are surely connected.

I now invite you to simply write down whatever has been keeping you up at night, or whatever decisions keep popping into your mind about your future.

At the end of the hour, or day, or night, collect those papers and/or post-it notes and centralize them all in one place where you can look at them together--either on a table top, a smart phone app, or in a computer file, for example. I will offer up navigational tools to help you bravely move through your fears into effective decision-making.

Perhaps equally valuable, I'll also point out false detours that could otherwise cost you time and money. Chief among them, strangely enough, is the media.

As if processing grief isn't overwhelming enough, the 24-hour financial news on television and radio can contribute to our feeling awash in the financial tide of information, yet clueless as to what to make of all of it. I mean, what the heck are we supposed to DO with all this information?

Somehow the proliferation of all this data causes especially vulnerable folks to suspect that they should **know** and remember this information, that they need to listen so they'll understand at least the basics, or even the language. Nonsense!

Remember that the financial media has one goal, and that goal generally is in direct conflict with your best individual or family interests and goals. Granted, the incredibly savvy media spends groups of zeroes to hook you into watching, listening, and reading what they promote; i.e., to keep your attention. So it's no wonder that we occasionally get sucked into their influence. Yet you cannot look to the media for your navigational investment advice.

What the DOW Jones Industrial Average or Standard & Poor's 500 (commonly referred to as the DOW and S&P500 respectively) closed at today is worthless information for your personal financial plan. We will detail how you can equip yourself to make better financial and personal decisions in later chapters, yet suffice it to say, watching CNBC or any other network isn't among them.

Summary Takeaway:

Write down what fears are keeping you up at night, which decisions are looming, and what questions you'd like answered. Fair warning: the media isn't your source for these answers.

Chapter 18
Financial Disasters to Avoid

(You may skip to Chapter 19 if you've hired, or have been convinced to hire, a fee-only CFP® (Certified Financial Planner™).

Sometimes knowing what I don't want leads me to what I do want and need. So while you may not be able to imagine or understand the value that a fee-only CFP® will provide, here are but a few examples of what some commissionable and fee-based salespeople have recommended to other widows, and the devastating effects of these recommendations.

It is in that spirit--so you can avoid similar setbacks--that I share these actual circumstances (names changed), suffered by people who later became either my clients, or clients of my fee-only CFP® associates.

Granted, estate and income tax laws invariably change, which would alter some of these examples' outcomes if they occurred today under current regulations. Yet similar omissions could hurt folks; hence the need to ensure that your plans comply with current law.

Long Term Care
A widow, Tammy, was sold a long-term care insurance policy and dutifully paid premiums on

it for over 14 years. On the application, Tammy listed her son as the person to receive premium notices in the event that she, the insured, did not pay the premiums; i.e., in the case the insured had an onset of dementia or Alzheimer's, for example, and didn't respond to the premium notices arriving in the mailbox.

Luckily Tammy didn't suffer from dementia, yet she moved, and apparently the insurance company wasn't informed of her move. So the premium notices were mailed to her old address and for whatever reason, went unforwarded to Tammy. When her premium wasn't received 30 days after the due date, the insurance company sent the backup reminder notice to her son, yet neither Tammy nor her agent had told the son that he was named as the secondary person appointed to receive back up premium notices, along with the rationale behind it. He disregarded the premium notice mailing, thinking it was junk mail, and his mother's long-term care policy lapsed.

Tammy now has cancer, and having lapsed her long-term care coverage has no way of reinstating the policy or obtaining new coverage. This potentially could result in her losing a bulk of her estate to spiraling attendant services and overall health care costs, should she be unable to complete 4 out of the 7 activities of daily living (ADLs as they're called), a typical requirement for long-term care insurance coverage to begin paying benefits.

Life Insurance

Upon the death of her husband, a widow named LuAnn was sold a two million dollar life insurance policy in her own name, in order to provide funds for the care of her young children should she die prematurely. Unfortunately, the ownership of the policy exacerbated LuAnn's estate size, so that when she died 15 years later, it was includable in her estate, subjecting her estate to $430,000 of estate taxes. This vastly reduced the monies that would otherwise have been available to her children.

This loss could have been averted had the agent taken the extra time to advise LuAnn to establish an irrevocable life insurance trust (referred to in the insurance industry as an ILIT) which would own the policy as of the date of the application, and thus remove this asset from her estate forever.

Life insurance death PROCEEDS are income-tax-free upon receipt, (which means that you pay no tax when you receive the death benefit monies); yet the OWNERSHIP of a life insurance policy is deemed ownership of an asset, much like the ownership of real estate or a financial asset. The lesser amount of either the policy's face amount, or the net death benefit payable, (should the policy have had an outstanding loan, for example) is includable in the decedents' estate for both federal and state estate tax purposes.

Variable Annuity

A 50-year-old widow named Vera was referred by her trusted CPA to his buddy, who visited Vera's home and promptly sold her a $500,000 variable annuity with a 10-year surrender period. The "buddy" made a commission of nearly $50,000 and won an all-expenses-paid trip-for-two to Maui, Hawaii as a result of the sale.

Meanwhile, Vera needed substantial cash for living expenses, so she had to withdraw income immediately. She also had to withdraw income over the 12 years until her pension and Social Security benefits began, subjecting a portion of each of her annual withdrawals to a hefty and senseless 8% surrender penalty.

Homeowners' Insurance

A widow named Helen was sold a homeowner's policy that didn't include a replacement cost rider on the contents of her home. During a lightning storm Helen's 10-year-old TV and a computer were both struck by lightning, rendering them useless. The insurance company claims adjuster depreciated her TV and computer to the extent that her claim check was only $180. But it could have covered the purchase of both a new TV and a new computer, had the agent included a very nominally priced replacement cost rider on Helen's contents.

Group Life Insurance

A woman named Toni risked losing her husband's group life insurance after he was diagnosed with cancer and had to leave his long-term job. Toni was so preoccupied with the caretaking of her husband, that while she faintly remembered that his group benefits changed when he quit working, she didn't understand the details.

She realized she wasn't able to handle both her caregiving role and attend to their family's finances, so she hired me as her Certified Financial Planner™. In reviewing her documents, I discovered that the deadline for conversion of her husband's life insurance was only three days away. I downloaded the conversion forms from the Internet and drove them to their home, where I got his signature on the forms. That same afternoon I mailed the signed forms to the company, via overnight mail, requiring a signature-return-receipt. Otherwise she would have surely missed the deadline. Her husband died 3 months later, and indeed the $140,000 death benefit was paid.

Unsuitable Commissionable Sale

A widow named Val was the primary beneficiary on four separate variable annuity contracts owned by her late husband, Al. Al died in early November, and the annuity salesperson visited Val two weeks later to obtain Al's death certificate and signed claim paperwork to submit to the issuing company for the payout checks. The week of Thanksgiving, the annuity salesperson delivered the death benefit payout checks to Val, and instructed her to write him equal dollar new checks, payable to a different variable annuity company. Why? In order to sell her a new variable annuity with another huge commission, payable to him!

- First, Val's receipt of all of the four death benefit proceeds entailed significant income tax ramifications because a bulk of the death proceeds represented ordinary income and was thus income taxable. Hence, Val was catapulted into the highest federal and state income tax bracket in the year of Al's death. Specifically, Val owed an additional $72,000 in federal income taxes and an additional $9,600 in state income taxes because of this agent's greedy blunder. (Point of clarification: the original amount invested in this after-tax variable annuity is called tax *basis*, and that was not taxable income to her upon receipt. Yet all the earnings since the date of purchase are considered ordinary taxable income.) Clearly, any reputable insurance company will hold a beneficiary's death proceeds in an interest-bearing account for at least 90 days and many will do so for 180 days or longer. Since Al's death occurred in November, holding Val's proceeds could have pushed the receipt of some or even a bulk of the taxable monies into the following tax year, minimizing both the federal and state income taxes that Val owed.

- Second, the agent earned another huge commission on the sale of a new annuity. But in fact, IF what the widow would have needed was an annuity (which it was not), Al's annuities could have been transferred into Val's name without incurring any fees or charges whatsoever.

Incomplete Beneficiary Designation

A life insurance agent sold a large life policy to a man we'll call Stan, writing the following words in the beneficiary box on the application: "Sarah, wife." Sadly, three years later, Stan and his wife Sarah were both killed instantly in a car accident. The coroner listed Sam's time of death as 8:04pm and Sarah's time of death as 8:05pm on their respective death certificates, resulting in the husband's assets passing into his wife's estate, where they were subjected to the processing and taxation of two estates.

Had the insurance agent instead written: "Sarah, wife, if she survives the insured for a period of 30 days, otherwise the children born of, or legally adopted by the marriage of the insured and said wife" (or similar language to any secondary beneficiary after Sarah) Sam's life insurance proceeds could have passed directly to the contingent beneficiary, without double legal fees and additional estate taxation.

Net Unrealized Appreciation

A recently retired widow named Sally was convinced by a commissionable agent to **roll over** her entire company 401(k) plan balance to a high-commission IRA variable annuity. The agent never bothered to ask Sally if she would need any ready funds, nor did he notice how her 401(k) plan was invested. Rather, he rationalized that she should take control of her own money now that she had left the company's employ, and encouraged her to give the money to him to manage for "safety." He apparently repeatedly asked Sally if she wanted the **security** of having a monthly check in her mailbox, inferring, of course, that this product was the only one that could provide such a monthly check, when any number of financial products could have done so.

Dutifully, Sally signed the agent's forms and transferred her entire balance directly from her former employer's company's 401(k) plan to that agent's employer, ABC life insurance company, to purchase the highest percentage commissionable IRA variable annuity *du jour*.

A month afterwards, Sally hired me as her CFP® to advise her on next steps of her retirement, since she was contemplating some extensive travel. She produced her old 401(k) statement to me; showing that 49% was invested in mutual fund-like sub-accounts and 51% was invested in her former company's stock. She relayed how proud she was to have worked for that company for 26 years, during which time the company stock price had more than **tripled**! Sally's 401(k) balance had ballooned as a result of that. But unfortunately when Sally rolled the entire 401(k) balance over into the salesman's recommended variable annuity IRA, she lost out on utilizing a little-known strategy called net unrealized appreciation (or NUA in industry jargon).

The NUA provision allows 401(k) investors to segregate their company stock portion from their non-company stock portion, creating 2 separate accounts. The NUA account (that which holds the company stock) is eligible to receive favorable tax treatment upon sale.

Specifically, Sally's company stock 401(k) account should have been segregated into such an account and then as she needed cash distributed to her, those assets would have been sold, qualifying for the much lower special NUA tax treatment (i.e., capital gains on the portion in excess of the trustee's cost basis, as compared with the much higher ordinary income tax rate).

Moreover, the normally required 1-year-and-1-day holding period to qualify for **long-term** capital gains is ALSO waived in NUA cases! This means Sally could have literally sold part or all of her company stock account the next day, and by virtue of the NUA favorable tax treatment, been eligible for the **long-term capital gains** tax rate. For Sally this was 15%, versus her ordinary income tax rate of 35%--a 20% tax rate differential!

In Sally's case, because she was not advised to utilize NUA, she was forced to pay an additional and totally unnecessary $8,400 in income taxes on the monies she withdrew to eliminate some outstanding debt and to fund her travel plans.

To add insult to injury, Sally was now holding a variable annuity product, which was NOT suitable for her needs. (While I pointed out that Sally's agent could have been held financially accountable for selling an unsuitable product, Sally didn't want to "press it," to use her exact words, since that agent was recommended by Sally's friend.)

Secondly, except for perhaps one circumstance, rare as it is--electing an accelerated death benefit rider for an uninsurable person--one should never invest individual retirement account (IRA) monies into a tax-deferred annuity, since the IRA itself is tax-sheltered. Think of it like putting one tax umbrella over another one, a redundancy for sure. Also, the expenses of a variable annuity are excessive, compared to investing those sums into institutional no-load mutual funds or ETFs (exchange traded funds) the latter two being among the lowest cost products available. Remember, lower investment costs translate into higher returns for you!

Suffice it to say, there are lots of horror stories and examples of situations where "had you only known" could have saved you significant money and heartache.

A commission-rewarded salesperson is not likely to explain all the nuances of a financial product (such as the excessively high fees and protracted surrender period), or take the time to educate the client on myriad solutions to a problem, if he or she can make a quick sale and scurry off to the luxury destination award trip they win by having sold these very commission-laden products. Such products are usually life insurance policies and annuities, yet more recently also include reverse mortgages.

Lest you perceive my casting a pall over every single commission-paid agent alive, these agents are simply not trained to provide other-than-commissionable product knowledge. That's their limit of expertise. I caution you to not leap to trusting that they are acting in your best interest, however kindly they may treat you.

Most likely they don't have any idea what your best interest is, or remotely how to provide services towards that end. They are not trained in financial planning nor do they have access to the myriad no sales load, razor-thin expenses product options that exist.

Summary Takeaway:

Eliminate huge unrecoverable expenses by working with a professional who does not profit from selling you commissionable financial product(s); i.e., a fee-only CFP®. If you see "Securities offered through…" on their business card/stationery, it's a commissioned agent.

Chapter 19
Why Pay the "Widow Tax?"

A widow needs to prepare to handle all of her purchases--not just the financial ones--with respectful caution and preparedness. Unfortunately, some unscrupulous sales people view widows as vulnerable and an easy target to sell to. This abuse costs widows untold sums of money and is commonly referred to as the "widow tax." You may have heard of the "gender tax" which costs women way too much as well, yet the "widow tax" can exact a double whammy with regard to the extra amounts that widows are often quoted. So be watchful and attentive!

Each widow can guard against such sales pressure by always stating, "I'll have to think about this purchase/proposal for a few days/weeks," and taking the salesperson's phone number, promising to call them back if and when you may wish to proceed.

Seldom is there a deal that isn't also available tomorrow or next week, or at a completely different store, regardless of how forcefully and urgently the sales person states their claim about "a limited time only" deal.

IF possible, take with you a man, who is knowledgeable on the item you are purchasing.

He will act as another set of eyes and ears; often elevating the tone of the sales interaction. As ridiculous as it may seem, the mere presence of a man will save women (and widows) money on most major purchases.

Incidentally, this problem also affects all single women, even though it's most commonly referred to as a "widow tax." The fact that particularly male salespeople think that women don't know the technical aspects of most major purchases causes too many of them to fast-talk women in a way that they wouldn't approach or speak to men.

Regrettably, I have personal evidence that occurred when I purchased my last brand new BMW, before I turned 50 years of age. I walked into several dealerships on a Saturday, dressed in jeans and a golf shirt, and was summarily ignored by over six sales people. I intentionally looked at several of the cars on the show room floor and read a few of the window price stickers. Eventually I was approached by a male salesperson who appeared as if he'd drawn the short straw, lamely asking if he could help me. Yet when a male customer entered the showroom, our conversation was cut short. He attended to the man while I became invisible.

I had researched everything about the BMW I was interested in buying, and had a very technical question about the slip differential. I asked my question to a total of four sales people at four different dealerships. No one knew the answer immediately, so I asked them to get back to me. Only one salesman called me back, and I bought the car from him.

Personal experience has taught me to do research on the product or service that I am buying. (This is, of course, much easier these days, with the Internet and even Smart Phones' abilities to serve up competitive pricing and information within seconds.) Knowledge is power, so having done your research you, too, will know whether the salesperson knows their stuff--features and price--versus just being a good talker.

One way to do this research on a computer is to simply type out your question directly into the search box of www.Google.com. In other words, move your mouse and cursor to the left-most space of your Internet service search box, often accompanied by a picture of a magnifying glass, regardless of whether it is Internet Explorer, Safari, Firefox, Chrome, or whatever. Then for instance, type in "what is the price of a GE Profiles dishwasher?"

Alternatively, if you own an Apple iPhone you could also ask Siri the same question. To ask Siri, you simply depress the circular button at the bottom of your iPhone for a second or two, and (presuming you've turned Siri on in your settings and then general menu) you can speak your question, "What is the price of a GE Profiles dishwasher?" or "Where can I buy a dishwasher?" into the microphone on your iPhone. Siri's answer will immediately appear on your screen, quite possibly asking if you want her to give you directions, or if you want her to call that store now; voila!

If, however, you have no Internet connection, simply get the specific manufacturer and model number of the item you wish to price and/or purchase, and make a series of phone calls to competitor stores that carry such merchandise. Ask if that item may be on special sale with them today, or will they be running a special sale soon? Get the price for that item as well as what service terms they may offer, either for free or for an extra charge.

May I suggest that you both look and sound informed when you venture into physical stores? Carry a pen and a clipboard or small notebook with specs of what you're looking for, and start out with something like this: "I was looking to upgrade my refrigerator with a more energy-efficient model, and perhaps an ice dispenser on the door, yet don't want to spend more than $1,000 on it; what could you suggest?" This sets the stage much differently than simply sauntering into a showroom with your purse slung over your shoulder.

The salesperson's answer will dictate whether you will question them further, and, eventually, whether you can trust them to be telling you valuable information about your purchase. Then, and only then, do you talk price. To repeat: avoid price discussions and bargaining until you've selected a salesperson with whom you have developed a rapport, with whom you feel comfortable.

Things do go wrong at times. If, for instance, the delivery people announce on the spot, "No ma'am, we have no service order to remove your old appliance" even though you know removal was a condition your salesperson promised when you purchased the new unit, you can feel confident picking up the telephone to connect with your salesperson, or that salesperson's supervisor, to immediately rectify the situation at hand.

In order to be sure of reliable ongoing service after your purchases, you should take the following precautions before you buy:

1. Inquire as to whether the quoted price would include delivery of the item and/or disposal of your current item if you're buying a replacement unit. Ask what that store's return policy is, specifically asking if there is a "restocking fee" and if so, what amount, or percentage, that fee represents of the purchase price, and,

2. Get the complete written terms of the product or service warranty that comes with the item. Added years of coverage or added component warranties represent huge sources of additional commission for retail clerks, so beware of being sold an unnecessary extra-charge warranty. (Your credit card may also automatically double the product warranty; check it out.)

While warranties are often a great idea, unless you intend to register the purchase within a few hours of arriving home and/or have an organized system for filing--paper or electronic--forget extra-charge warranties. You don't need more upset in your life about not being able to find the receipt and/or warranty papers, or berating yourself later for not registering your purchase.

Have you ever wondered just how to do stuff? Like fixing basic things that go wrong, or how to use a product that you found on your husband's workbench? Here's a website that is the best source I know to get step-by-step instructions on how to do almost anything: www.YouTube.com.

Seriously, you type in whatever you are curious about, and voila, it serves you up several or several hundred videos, often homemade ones shot by amateurs, yet these are the very people to break down industry jargon and speak English (and other languages, of course) about how to fix stuff, or use tools, or make cool projects.

I just typed in "how to open plastic containers" and up popped four videos--the first one I clicked on showed a woman using a handheld can opener to pierce through that tough plastic. I learned something now that will save me both time and injury in the future.

You can also use this site in order to get even a cursory idea of just how serious your home repair may be to fix. Let's say your sink has a leak; water is dripping from your pipes underneath your sink. Instead of just calling the plumber and stating in a passive voice, "my sink sprung a leak, can you fix it?" I recommend that you type in "how to fix a leaky sink" and see what appears as possible resources.

While you may not choose to follow the instructions that appear by repairing the leak yourself, you will at least now know the vernacular to use when you call the plumber, or local handyman. Like, "my sink water trap is leaking; I'm hoping it's just a faulty O ring, yet can you look at it?" That way, the plumber knows better than to bill you for a ton of parts and/or labor for what sounds like a small job. You will still review his/her detailed invoice and question any part that seems unnecessary.

I must warn you, however, that you could find yourself on this website for hours on end, so budget your time and then learn away. This is another reason the Internet is so important in our lives; sites like these bring common sense information and helpful tips into our otherwise complicated worlds, and for free no less!

Finally, **compile a list of trustworthy repair people.** Cull a list of names and phone numbers or email addresses and websites of repair people known to you, and then ask family and friends for recommendations to fill in the gaps. An electrician, a plumber, a handyperson, a computer whiz, a painter, a car mechanic, a pest control service, and an air conditioning and heating person are among the more important areas of specialty to cover.

Summary Takeaway:

Being forewarned is being forearmed to prevent being charged extra for products and services as a woman (and especially a widow). And take a man to the store when you are ready to purchase your item; it will likely save you money, sometimes big bucks!

Chapter 20
Where Will I Live?

It is important to consider carefully whether you will remain in your home/apartment/condo/co-op or move to another. Whether you will purchase or rent a different house or apartment are considerations that need to be weighed, along with the timing of each of these decisions.

Since the process of downsizing or even moving into another similarly-sized home or living space is fraught with emotion (not to mention a great deal of physically and mentally exhausting work) one would be wise to temper the speed with which they have to act.

If, for example, you wish to move out of your current home, and if finances allow, it may be prudent to secure the new housing arrangement a month before your move date. This would allow you time to renovate the new home or apartment in order to get it exactly as you want it before you move in.

Additionally this option allows for your taking time to begin sorting out your files and storage areas, followed by the contents of each room. It's ideal if you can allow yourself ample time to do this in an orderly fashion, earmarking (and physically attaching names to) specific items, or boxes of items, that you wish to give to various family and friends.

Remember, although you reserve the right to change your mind later, simply starting on this task is laudable. The first step is the hardest, so enlist a trusted friend or family member to help, if possible. Afterword, the task becomes more "do-able" with each successive step.

The decision about where you may choose to live involves money, feelings, memories, opportunities and challenges. Where to live may well depend on your health, the location of your kids, relatives, or friends, and your ability to afford a home in an area that suits you. Basic decisions include whether to own your own home, or to own or rent a condo--be it permanent or seasonal--or to apply for admittance into a senior community's independent living program or an assisted living community.

More living arrangements are being created each day, so be sure to check out all of your options, even if you fear you can't afford them. (I often have to assure my widowed clients that they can indeed afford much of what they perhaps secretly wish to do, because their fear tends to limit their possibilities.) That's another reason to enlist a fee-only CERTIFIED FINANCIAL PLANNER™: each of us have the tools to run probability analysis reports, called Monte Carlo simulations, that factor in the anticipated expenses--both in today's dollars

as well as inflation-adjusted expense numbers--
to show whether or not one can afford a
particular standard of living, and for how long.

If you've owned your own home, you are
familiar with paying property taxes and
contracting out for your yard work and general
maintenance. Be advised that the maintenance
for yards, sidewalks and often driveways, are all
wrapped up in one monthly fee for most
condominium and co-op complexes, so all of
your maintenance is handled by someone else.
And that's one less thing for you to handle.
However, these costs escalate over the years,
and the amount of the increase is virtually out
of your control unless you wish to influence
costs by serving on the board of directors.
Absent that, it's best to build in a cushion for
increases in your monthly housing expenses.

Finally, if your mobility is currently
challenged or you anticipate its becoming more
challenged, research independent or assisted
living communities. A motorized wheel chair,
or a jazzy as they're sometimes called, can
enable folks to transport themselves throughout
their single level homes or apartments, as well
as to and from the parking lot or dining room
and elsewhere in a community housing facility.

Adult communities and assisted living
facilities offer a built-in society with which you
could meld to some degree, all the while
maintaining your existing, established
friendships. They offer the best of both worlds,

some new friends and activities to complement your old friends and pastimes.

Pets

While some widows already have pets, others do not, and they may wonder whether they should get a pet. While I realize that some pets can be a very welcome greeter when you arrive home, can cuddle up to you in your favorite chair or bed and provide company, I also know that pets require attentive daily care and feeding; and pet food and vet bills do add up. I simply caution you about taking on another responsibility at a time when your energy or finances may be tapped-out.

Growing up on a farm, I understand the responsibility of caring for animals. Yet as I write this, I can just feel the tsunami of responses from pet lovers attesting to the love of their pet(s) and claims that "it's nothing to care for a pet."

Okay, having pets or not is an individual choice, yet know that with regard to housing choices, there may be pet restrictions varying from no pets, to pets below a certain weight limit. Be sure to check these out.

Summary Takeaway:

Housing choices are highly personal, but you can rely on your fee-only CFP® to determine what you can afford and what may be the most suitable choice for you.

Chapter 21
Nurturing My Core Essence

Your authentic self has changed, if nothing more than by your role changing from being a wife to that of a widow. To add to the complexity, your authentic self may have been dusty or buried during some stints of your marriage.

When my friend's husband of a decade died, she exclaimed to me, "He did everything; how will I live?"

I listened respectfully as she continued spewing out her worries. I then asked her specifically what John did, and she regaled a very long list. When she was finished identifying these tasks and services I paused and quietly reminded her that I knew her before she met John. And before she and John were married, she supported herself, drove herself places, cooked meals, and grocery shopped. I assured her that in time, she could certainly resume doing all, or almost all, of these things again.

I still remember the disbelief on her face as she received this information from me. She knew it was factual, yet it took her a long while to assimilate these truths so that she could begin to believe in herself again.

I assured her that regaining these skills would indeed take time, yet there was no stopwatch measuring her progress minute-by-minute or even day-by-day.

I encouraged her to chunk these tasks down into bite-sized pieces and write those on pieces of paper attached to her frig door, her bathroom mirror, her desk and her kitchen cabinets. I suggested messages like these:

- I am a trained nurse, I can support myself.

- I am an effective problem solver, I can do this.

- I am a good driver, I can transport myself where I want, and need, to go.

- I am a good friend; I can rekindle friendships that may have grown apart, as well as meet new friends.

Journaling or keeping a diary is both healthy and therapeutic as well as a physical reference to look back upon to **see** your progress. In turn, journal entries actually serve to prove that growth has occurred. It's most helpful to see proof of what's already been achieved, perhaps when your focus was somewhere else, like on basic survival. But first and foremost, journaling is good for your soul. It is a way to express emotions--positive and negative--as vividly and descriptively as you wish.

Often widow's journal entries move swiftly across a whole range of emotions; it's almost like a band of emotions are all jockeying to be heard, to "get out" and be expressed. There's a logjam at the entrance, yet as soon as one feeling is expressed, there's room to recognize and express the next emotion, and then the next and the next. What may have felt like too daunting a task--to untangle all the pent-up emotions--becomes quite natural and simple with writing even a few sentences each day.

If you don't prefer to write, and have access to a smart phone or an Apple iPad, or similar device, you can now activate the microphone feature, and either speak into an email which you will send to yourself, or into a notes application. The transcriptions are generally very accurate: at least enough to allow you to express your feelings and recognize them later, without requiring constant access to a pen and pad.

There will be plenty of time to decide whether you wish to share any parts of, or your entire journal, with anyone else--yet for now, I encourage you to just keep writing or speaking.

Many widows decide to write blog entries that chronicle their feelings and experiences with the express intent for others to see their posts and benefit by them. Sympathy in numbers is powerful, surely. Reading others' blog posts can be an effective way to reach out and connect with another person, and even to start a dialogue.

Here are some of my favorite blogs and sites, most of them written by widows:

> www.soaringspirits.org/resources/blog-roll/
> www.freshwidow.blogspot.com/p/blogroll.html

- www.abigailcarter.com
- www.widowswearstilettos.com
- www.facebook.com/freshwidow
- www.facebook.com/LivingWithLoss OneDayAtATime
- www.facebook.com/modernwidows club?fref=pb&hc_location=profile_ browser
- www.facebook.com/2damnyoung?fr ef=pb&hc_location=profile_browser
- www.facebook.com/grieftheunspoke n?fref=pb&hc_location=profile_bro wser
- www.facebook.com/TheWidowsJour ney?fref=pb&hc_location=profile_b rowser
- www.grief.com
- www.calebwilde.com
- www.theloombafoundation.org/

Summary Takeaway:

Connect with someone who knew you before you met your husband for reminders of your essence and proven capabilities. Journal or speak and record your innermost thoughts; they will serve as both therapy and your proof of how far you've progressed.

Chapter 22
Guilt, Anger and Forgiving

Often widows harbor anger and guilt for reasons including, yet not limited to, the following:

- Anger that he up and died, leaving you alone,

- Guilt you weren't there at the exact moment of his death,

- Anger at God for allowing him to die,

- Guilt that you never said goodbye,

- Anger that he was careless,

- Guilt that you had argued that day,

- Anger that all he did was work; he had no work-life balance,

- Guilt that you'd withheld sex,

- Anger that he racked up debts,

- Guilt that you couldn't be a better caregiver,

- Anger that he had an affair,

- Guilt that you had an affair,

- Anger that the driver lived,

- Guilt that you failed to learn valuable life skills,
- Anger that you have to raise the kids alone,
- Guilt that you kept secrets,
- Anger that he nixed the life insurance,
- Guilt that you didn't say "I love you" on the morning of the day he never returned home,
- Anger that he suffered, dying a slow painful death.

Forgiving such guilt and anger may sound impossible, yet our lives depend on nothing less. Forgiveness is for **us**, not him, or anyone whom we believe wronged us. It is our own health that is compromised so long as we hold onto our bitterness.

And to set the record straight, he (and you) didn't "lose the battle" with an extended illness; you both fought valiantly to the end of the illness. Neither he nor you are "losers."

While you no doubt find yourself hoping he'll walk through that door, phone or text you, at some level you know that you must now live wrapped tightly in your memories of him. Whether that's wearing his clothes, sleeping on his side of the bed, cuddling his fluffy bathrobe, spraying his cologne in your bathroom or car, mimicking his favorite gesture to you, or cooking his favorite meal, you'll cry your way through the pain, the anger, and the abject sadness of knowing you have to rely on memories of the past.

When you are able to decide to release this part of your pain, that indeed he died and that won't change, then and only then can your psyche accept the instantaneous and then sustained relief and lightness that acceptance and ultimately forgiveness inevitably brings.

I encourage you to talk with your late husband, telling him everything that's on your heart and mind. Rage at him, talk tenderly to him, cry, wail, or moan your grief and fears. Then listen to, or be aware of, his receiving that information, noticing the guidance and clarity of spirit and mind that so often will follow.

A practice called tapping has also provided relief for myriad widows, or anyone suffering stress, anger or extreme emotions. Nick Ortner's 2013 book, *The Tapping Solution*, Hay House, Inc., explains EFT—emotional freedom techniques--that actually interrupt our body's stress reactions through a combination of psychology and Chinese acupressure and you can do it yourself, anytime, anywhere. It's so insanely simple yet I, too, have found significant relief after tapping.

Summary Takeaway:

Release resentments, replacing "woulda, coulda, shoulda" with "I forgive you, I forgive me, we both know now, we did the best we could and it was good."

Chapter 23
I Release My Partner

Often a widow may need permission to stop crying every day…believing that if she doesn't continue to cry, either her husband won't remember she loves him or her friends may doubt that she loved him. This feeling is as powerful as it is because it is largely subconscious. Once we audibly state the feeling, however, it becomes far less gripping.

I know that when I was coaching Molly, a grieving client whose husband had died three weeks earlier, she said, through panicked sobs, "If I stop crying every day, I fear he'll think I didn't love him." I listened in heartfelt silence. She looked up at me through her tears, clearly eager for answers. After a respectable silence I asked, "Well, how would you feel about our asking your husband right now, if he knows you love him?"

She stopped crying, and stared straight at me, with a combination of disbelief and then budding hope in her eyes. I stared back at her, and frankly I think we were both wondering how that would look and sound.

I proceeded with words that were truly given to me: "I believe your beloved husband, Ray, is sitting at the right hand of God now,

and knows far more than we know. Let's ask
him, shall we?" She nodded. "Ray, do you know
just how much Molly loved and loves you?"
Silence. I continued, "Will you still know how
very much Molly loved and loves you if she
doesn't cry every single day?" More silence.

Then Molly stated with quiet certainty, "I
feel Ray's presence, and I believe he knows that
I love him more than anything."

"Certainly," I concurred, "and further, I feel
that he is not only releasing you, he is urging
you to take the next steps in your grief journey,
crying when you feel the need, yet also taking
care of yourself as lovingly as he did. Do you
feel that?"

"Yes!" she exclaimed. Then she added, "Ray
was a hugger, may I have a hug?" And hug we
did.

Let's decipher this event in the hope that it
can bring you relief too.

1. Face and move through any "survivor
    guilt." Your life and especially your friends'
    lives DO go on after your beloved's death.
    However cruel that may feel, it is reality.
    The sooner you are able to begin venturing
    into your new life--however **not chosen**
    that new life is, of course--the sooner you
    will feel some relief. Little steps are all I'm
    talking about here; little progress steps--
    getting dressed in the morning, consciously
    taking three deep breaths and slowly
    exhaling, eating at least one healthy meal

each day, getting some exercise, even if that's just stretching, and stepping outside into the fresh air, possibly taking a short walk.

2. These self-care steps do NOT mean that you will forget your husband, or that you don't love him, or that God got the order wrong and it should have been you. It simply means that there was only one name that you recognized in the obituaries, and it wasn't yours. So now what?

Seize the obligation to yourself, your beloved husband, your family, your community and perhaps to your Higher Power to find or re-create and fulfill your own unique reason for being, **your reason for living**.

This is exactly what's meant when most widows can eventually reflect on perhaps months or years of grief and declare, "It was the worst thing that ever happened to me, **AND** because of how I now live my life with full intention and how I treat other people, it was also the best thing that ever happened to me!"

They certainly DON'T mean they are **glad** they are widowed. They acknowledge they are indeed a member of a "club they didn't choose." Yet now they are called not only to exist, but to navigate the questions, and live forward as changed and still vibrant individuals.

In an eerie almost indescribable sort of way, they experience a heightened consciousness about life and about meaning. They admit feeling better by both giving to themselves and giving to others. So, yes, full in the knowledge that your husband still loves you and you will always deeply love and sorely miss him, you step forward, which is **exactly** what he would have wanted.

Summary Takeaway:

Thank your husband that you can make deliberate progress now precisely because you trust that in his love for you, he wouldn't have it any other way.

Chapter 24
Dusting Off My Courage

Tony Robbins states that we should compile at least three possible solutions or options to solve any problem. One choice is far too limiting, two choices may infer, "I'm darned if I do, and darned if I don't," but three choices offer us real opportunities to vet the situation, feel our feelings around selecting any of the choices, and really home in on what FEELS **best**.

While initially daunting to many widows, the abundance of new choices can eventually feel wonderful! Take for example, the widow who may have been caring for her ill husband months or years before he died. That caregiving wife's duties probably precluded her from enjoying some of life's simple luxuries, such as these:

- Getting in her car for a country drive,

- Buying herself a special bouquet of flowers,

- Driving to her favorite ice cream stand to enjoy an ice cream cone,

- Visiting the grand kids, and/or

- Meeting her girlfriend(s) for lunch.

Caretaking kept her out of the regular circulation of life in many respects, focused narrowly on keeping her beloved comfortable and feeling loved, ensuring he took the proper meds, shuttling him to doctors, and so forth.

If you were a caretaker to your husband before his death, you face an additional hurdle (over and above that which survivors face when husbands died suddenly). Best to recognize and acknowledge that, so you can plan how to dust off and incorporate certain choices back into your everyday routine of life. Your new choices may include these:

- Being able to go to the late movie,

- Arriving home at midnight,

- Visiting out-of-town family & friends,

- Accepting a second invitation on a weekend,

- Entertaining in your home--perhaps because now the hospital bed has been moved out and you have access to a new room.

Speaking of which, you may now wish to establish a dark room so you can develop your own photography, or a sewing room, or a crafts/hobby/scrapbooking room, where you can build or buy shelving or containers to organize your supplies. Or you can dedicate a room to yoga, meditation, music or exercise, perhaps purchasing your own musical instruments and/or treadmill or elliptical.

If you have otherwise preserved the room where your husband slept, you will eventually be led to the exact time to reconsider new uses for that space--either choices that *include* his memory, or that infuse that room with a wholly different energy. You can do both, you know. Start out with re-imagining that room in one fashion, and then making that happen, with an open mind to changing everything should you have a different idea later.

Options are empowering; allow yourself to think and feel through various options in every facet of your life. Yes, you may automatically and perhaps emphatically say, "Oh, I'll never do that" or "are you kidding me, that's totally out of the question."

But then a funny thing happens; you're talking with a friend who has done just that thing that you've just sworn you'd NEVER do, and it has worked for them. That gives you an opening to question your earlier beliefs and statements and stand in your own power, which includes the power to change your mind without berating yourself.

Ahh…a woman's power to change her mind rings familiar…yet I invite you to experience this without the self-deprecation and the self-judgment that too often follows society's reference to "women's changing their minds."

I'm an advocate of options, many options, which allows me to segue into my mantra that money is merely a tool that buys options or choices. All the more reason to gain an

understanding of and mastery of our money--
how we want to use and direct it, now and in
the future.

Summary Takeaway:

*Now that you have a window of time and your CFP® to
give you the financial all-clear, dust off your courage to
either consider new opportunities or revisit old customs,
experiences or habits that brought you joy.*

Chapter 25
You Bet I'm Connected

While connecting can happen easily via telephone, sometimes we just don't feel quite up to making a phone call. Luckily, more passive relating can happen very easily by using our computer and the Internet. If you don't have a computer, or haven't a clue as to how to turn a computer on, let alone use it, then perhaps a course at the local library or civic center or university may be helpful.

This is a great example of an area of life where some more mature women don't even know what we don't know about the computer or the Internet. In other words, just what can I learn or access on the Internet may be logical questions that emerge as people are all abuzz about the Internet. A class at the local library or university on computing and the Internet will inform you as to some of the possibilities that exist to save you time or money, or simply entertain you. That may be the best time investment you can make in order to stay current on the pictures that your friends, children, grandchildren, or nieces and nephews are posting on Facebook, for example.

I recommend that you check out Internet sites like www.Pinterest.com which is most popular with women of all ages as a venue for sharing various items of interest--anything from pictures to quotes to recipes to fashion to raising kids to vacations to health to empowering to funny videos. The idea here is to connect. Many widows' barriers to connection with others, and particularly with other women, are old messages that need to be swept out of our brains.

In UCLA's study entitled *Friendship Among Women*, Drs. Klein and Taylor found that women supporting women is healthy physiologically, due to the oxytocin release that naturally occurs when women share and bond with each other as a stress-coping behavior. (Males, on the contrary, deal with their stress by isolating from each other.) So, it's proven that women's connecting is healthy in addition to fun; fancy that!

Why not throw yourself a birthday party? I recommend inviting only singles, as this gives a whole new opportunity to connect with myriad other singles in your community, or within your circle of family and friends. Suggest on the invitation that everyone brings one food item--designate types of food if you wish by making a game of it. For instance, state on the invitation, according to the first letter of your first name,

- **A** bring an appetizer,
- **B** bring beer, birch beer, or bagels, your choice,

- **C** bring cupcakes or cheese & crackers,
- **D–G** bring a non-alcoholic drink,
- **H–I** bring ice cream,
- **M–P** bring a meat or other protein dish,
- **R–S** bring a salad & salad dressing,
- **T** bring toppings for ice cream,
- **V** bring veggies,
- **W** bring wine,
- Any other letter, bring a surprise.

Indicate the specific games you'll have available to play, such as Pictionary, Scrabble, Chinese checkers, Dominos, Pick-up Sticks, and Wii, naming which of these you own. Alternatively I've shared side-splitting laughter playing the game called Heads Up!--app available on the iPhone and other Smart Phones. Naming any of these or other specific games will stoke the excitement and engage people to RSVP early.

Preparing for this party may also be a great excuse to get your home ready for company. You do the sorting, and hire a good cleaning service to help.

Summary Takeaway:

Take the risk of connecting; it's well worth it!

Chapter 26
It's Fun to Give & Receive

Whether you are giving or receiving a smile, a knowing glance, a hug, or advice, it's fun. Refocusing attention on folks or causes outside our families is not only healthy for them; it is healthy for us too! It is in giving to others that we humans erase depression and lift our own mood.

Because funding has been slashed from charities, you will be VERY much appreciated if you are able to give a donation of your time or money to your favorite cause(s). There is so much need in our fragile world. Where is a glaring volunteer void that you can easily and joyfully fill in your community? See how your skills and interests align with opportunities at www.volunteermatch.org.

Some charities offer travel opportunities to participate in research projects. In this fashion, you could choose where-in-the-world-you'd-like-to-travel, and then research the service trip opportunities. Websites include:

> ➢ www.globalvolunteers.org
> ➢ www.starfishvolunteers.com

But it is also vital to learn how to receive. Learning to receive, you say? Yes, indeed, receiving is a laudable and most valuable lesson for widows, as it is for all mature human beings.

My favorite example of a widow learning to receive involved my Aunt. She was moving into an assisted living facility and organized a yard sale to sell the contents of her home. I drove to her home the day before and said I wanted to help affix price stickers to her yard sale items. She said confidently, "I can do that!" to which I answered, "I know you can, AND I want to give you a gift by helping you attach the price stickers." She stopped, looked softly into my eyes and said, "I guess if you want to give, then I better learn how to receive"--to which I nodded and kissed her on the cheek. We had a most productive and love-filled day together.

Summary Takeaway:

Paying it forward in any small or large way is perhaps one of the most selfless and fulfilling acts we can perform. Learning to receive graciously runs a very close second; practice both!

Chapter 27
Caregiving, Check! Oh, Me?

As a widow (or as a caregiver to your ill husband for weeks, months or years before he died), you now deserve to receive care--given both by yourself and by other friends and professionals.

You'll need to replenish your own energy and body and spirit, much like a car requires repairs after either having been in an accident or running continuously without regular service appointments.

While giving seems natural to most women, giving to ourselves requires that we hone our skill of receiving! The circle of life (and death) invariably involves receiving. Imagine if your husband couldn't receive from you; yet however difficult it may have been for him, most likely he did. Now you, too, can hurdle any of your previous blocks around receiving and take in new full measurements of love--from yourself and your friends and family.

For payments ranging from free to $50, you might consider any of the following:

• Escaping the world in a warm bubble bath surrounded by candles and soft classical harp or violin or piano music.

- Searching Groupon or other discount websites for a discount coupon for massage, mani-pedi or facial, and then USING each coupon. C'mon now, work with me here!

- Walking around your block on a sunny morning, whistling a familiar tune, whether you can whistle or not.

- Shopping for your favorite fragranced moisturizer cream and routinely rubbing it on after your morning or evening shower.

- Making a list of the movies you'd like to catch up on. Consider asking your friends what are the best movies they've watched in the last year, eliminating, for now, the films where one of the partners dies.

- Buying a small bouquet of flowers from the grocery store or farmer's market, to brighten your kitchen or living room or bedroom.

Physical activity is also generally thought to be great for both the body and the soul, yet it is smart to start by getting a complete physical exam with blood work from your physician BEFORE you begin an exercise program.

Since stress takes a huge toll on our health, and since we are now committed to replenishing ourselves to optimum health, the idea is to detect what metabolic or acid vs. alkaline levels may be the most out-of-balance.

I prefer visiting my naturopathic doctor and master herbalist, Dona Garofano, founder of Food For Thought (www.foodforthought-

healthstore.com) who does both dried blood
analysis and then muscle tests me on the
vitamins and minerals I am currently taking, to
see if I am assimilating both the vitamin or
mineral itself as well as that particular brand
properly.

While some supplement brands actually
contain harmful ingredients or fillers, landing
them on Dona's *Wall of Shame* for their false
advertising claims, other legitimate brands may
not be as effective for people with certain
different blood types. So what's helpful for your
friend may or may not be effective for you. Best
to be spending the money and time on what
your body can assimilate, right?

Whether we visit medical doctors or utilize
alternative medicine or a combination thereon,
let's all get on a plan to treat our biggest
imbalances first, and then take pro-active
preventative measures to better ensure our
health far into the future.

Summary Takeaway:

*The lesson for most of us is learning to receive graciously;
we must do it until it is second nature. And schedule a
physical check-up and blood work-up now.*

Chapter 28
I Plan to Last

A widow may well live several more decades, so it's best to get strong--physically and mentally--so those years can be as fulfilling as possible and lived independently on your terms, rather than perhaps needing special care such as a wheel chair or a walker. Attitude about retaining as much mobility as possible, and attention to diet and exercise, are key to increasing your life's options.

If you had truncated your activities and hobbies prior to your husband's death, you can now rejoin them as you're physically able, building up stamina--perhaps slowly at first, yet taking action day by day. Engaging a personal trainer to coach and cheerlead you in a wellness and strength program is a wise choice to both monitor your health and gain a partner in your quest and commitment to get strong or regain your strength.

We planners tend to toss the term longevity around, yet in the case you don't really understand it, the odds increase for your increased longevity, the older you are. It's quite logical when we break down the math, yet who thinks about this early in life? Taking measures to preserve our health right now are smart, and ultimately less costly financially and emotionally.

Here's a look at Longevity Risk:

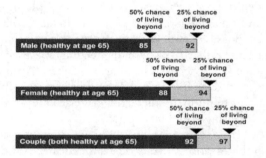

Longevity Odds

Derived from Wharton Financial Institutions Center Policy Brief: Personal Finance, Investing Your Lump Sum at Retirement by David F. Babbel and Craig B. Merrill. Pg. 4. August 14, 2007.

On the first line of this chart you will see that a healthy 65-year-old male has a 50% chance of living beyond age 85 and a 25% chance of living beyond age 92. On the second line we see that a healthy 65-year-old female has a 50% chance of living beyond age 88 and a 25% chance of living beyond age 94. Clearly, the longer a female (or male) lives, the longer she or he has the probability to live.

Summary Takeaway:

The longer we live, the better our chances of living a much longer life, the odds of which are enhanced by great family genes and self-care, diet and exercise. Invest in your health now; it'll likely pay dividends for years to come.

Chapter 29
Re-creating My Life

Expectations of doing this or that with your late husband have been dashed, yet you are still here--maybe existing rather than living right now, yet you are here. And you have a purpose while you are grieving and as you pass through your grief.

While it may sound insensitive for me to suggest, other widows have expressed such relief when they became intentional about acknowledging and expressing their gratitude for their lives, and those of their children, if they have them. Abraham Lincoln said, "Folks are usually about as happy as they make their minds up to be." Yes, ultimately our happiness is well within our control.

I invite you to develop, foster and nurture a huge dose of curiosity about your present and future. This may be done in a host of ways, chief among them **asking HOW questions of yourself**.

It is likely you've already passed through many of the WHY questions, which typically emerge immediately after the death. Yet the HOW questions are valuable too, in that they **move us through the strategy stage**, where more things get accomplished. Typical questions include the following:

- How will I maintain this house?

- How will I pay the mortgage or rent?

- How will I fund the kids' or grandkids' education?

- How will I spend my days, or nights?

- How will I fund my own retirement?

- How will I fit in with all of my married friends?

- How will I meet new friends?

I'll suggest a few hobbies here which may appeal to you, yet fill in the blanks with whatever interests you.

Cooking is something that often goes by the wayside, as one may not feel like cooking for themselves, choosing instead to eat a bowl of cereal for dinner. Somehow, the act of cooking seems to have connoted a necessity of eating with someone else. Yet I invite you to break out of that belief, if indeed it ever was yours.

One way to ease back into cooking is to take a cooking class, or watch a cooking show on television and follow their instructions in creating a new dish or embellishing an old recipe.

Sharing a recipe or even a funny story of a dish that flopped may also evoke your interest and that of your Facebook, Pinterest, or other-than-social media friends.

Reading is also essential to growing and learning. Consider joining a book club, so that you can discuss the books you read afterwards with folks you may, in time, call friends. In the meantime, this provides rich, quality social time with others.

Games/Puzzles can also be important. Playing bridge, cribbage or other card or board games, or Wii games, are all examples of how you can schedule fun with others, often with ZERO cost. Completing crossword and Sudoku puzzles also keeps our mind sharp!

Exercise is vital but the key is to make it fun, as an enjoyable building block to getting stronger and healthier. Tennis, golf, badminton, squash, racquetball, walking, pilates, stretching, yoga, and tai chi are all great activities, some of which can be done by yourself--with or without your favorite music piping through your ear buds or room--while others require a partner.

Summary Takeaway:

Ask and answer the "HOW will I move forward and shape my purpose?" questions, both with others and by myself. Re-create your life first with tentative tenacity, then with persistent resolve.

Chapter 30
Yes, I Will Create my Bucket List

What do you still want (or need) to do, before you die? I recommend that you start writing down every such idea--especially the hair-brained notions--keeping a magnetized tablet on your refrigerator perhaps, and a small notepad in your car, in your purse, on your night stand, and in your bathroom. Anywhere and everywhere, just so you can access them whenever you have a thought to record (and you KNOW how thoughts can and do invariably come to us in the shower or bath).

Smart phones now serve as information storage tools, too, since we can simply push a button, talk, and see the words transcribed right before our eyes. This makes dream building and creating bucket lists--heck, ANY list--effortless and fun.

Years ago two of my divorced, single women clients received a cancer diagnosis a day apart during the week of Easter. I was **deeply** saddened.

That night as I lie in bed it dawned on me how many frequent flier miles I had accrued, some of which could be used to fly my beloved and older aunts to my Florida condo for a reunion in the sun. I awakened excited, yet nonetheless dubious--the litmus test would be clearing it first with my hadn't-flown-in-5 years-88-year-old aunt. Ring, ring: "Aunt Janet, Hi, this is Debra and I have a hair-brained idea."

"Yeees?" she slowly queried.

"I thought you and the other aunts should escape Pennsylvania's winter weather and be my guests at my Florida condo in a couple of weeks; I'll fly you down on my miles; what do you think?" I held my breath.

Without a moment's hesitation, she retorted, "I'm pulling my suitcase out now!" This marks the 4th year that my aunts and I have fulfilled and commemorated that original hair-brained idea.

Because seeing a different setting other than one's home is often relaxing and/or exhilarating, I invite you to write down five trips you'd like to take in the next year. And then write down five more trips you'd like to line up for the following year.

If you are retired, or otherwise not working outside your home, you may be able to take advantage of www.lastminutetravel.com opportunities--cruises, airlines, hotels, etc., all of which offer terrific savings for people who book travel at the last minute. That boat, plane or hotel will be in operation tomorrow and the next day or week, regardless of whether it's sold out or not. So over and above the number they need to break even financially, any additional guests they can attract will represent pure profit. The prices are therefore often slashed to unbelievably low levels.

Here are a couple of ideas for stimulating good times:

1. Form a travel group consisting of friends or family and exchange lists of places you each want to travel to, so that everyone can keep an eye out for last-minute sales. There are travel-for-single groups, which can be located by searching the Internet or by reading about these in your local newspaper or local magazines. While many agencies offer single supplement options, here are three such websites that cater specifically to single travelers: www.singlestravelintl.com, www.worldtravelforsingles.com, www.solomatetravel.com.

2. Or think about this: how many times do your family members and friends draw a blank on what to give you for your birthday or the holidays? How about suggesting to them that you'd appreciate a paid subscription to your area or state magazine, which lists events and posts stories about places of interest? Or, if you love to hike or commune with nature, how about a year's membership that allows you unlimited access to any of the state parks in your state of residence? IF you have access to the Internet, simply search on memberships at state parks, and you'll be treated to a ton of enjoyable choices.

For now just list these sights, destinations and experiences without putting prices on them, or limiting yourself with the thought, "I couldn't afford that!" You will work later at prioritizing your expenditures, yet you need targets to aim for, especially now.

And if there is nothing that comes to your mind that you'd like to do, perhaps because you still feel so *empty* in your grief…or you're one of those people who never quite allowed themselves to daydream, or even dream, then you may want to start a scary, woo-woo thing like meditation to open up that side of yourself. It just might bring you inestimable pleasure and joy.

I have found Deepak Chopra's meditations particularly helpful in soothing my spirit. He's created the 21-day meditation experience, promoting healing, wellness and peace. Check out any of his websites, including www.chopra.com/community or his YouTube videos on meditation.

Summary Takeaway:

Amass a wish list of travel locations or experiences that you'd like to visit or know firsthand before you die. Then, if you wish company, determine which of your friends could join you on each experience.

Chapter 31
Back in the Driver's Seat

While this can also be interpreted correctly as a figurative statement, quite literally, widows need to get back into the driver's seat of their own car. If your car is your major mode of transportation, getting comfortable driving, and especially driving without a passenger, is great progress. If you haven't driven as much in recent years, take it as slowly as you would approach any skill that may be a bit rusty.

Start by driving around your neighborhood and on familiar roads only. Practice backing up and parallel parking on a cul-de-sac so you aren't distracted by other cars. This practice will retool your skills and **rebuild your confidence** to venture onto the busier streets, taking care to avoid traveling at rush hour if possible.

Rush hour travelers are typically in a hurry, which tends to heighten their stress levels. And when stress levels are heightened, people invariably act in a rude and inconsiderate manner, none of which you need to be exposed to right now. Rude drivers really don't mean to hurt, they are simply letting off steam, yet for you to receive that negativity isn't helpful. Do what you can to avoid those situations.

Because driving under the influence of grief is often all-consuming, plan on allowing plenty of time to drive to your destination. Allow for these possibilities:

- You might lose your way, make a wrong turn, and get lost or otherwise delayed.

- You might be thinking about something other than driving and potentially put yourself into harm's way.

If either of these happens to you when you are driving, I recommend that you pull off to the side of the road, or into a well-lit rest stop or restaurant, and gather yourself. That may take the form of simply meditating for a few minutes, saying a centering prayer, taking some sips of water, giving yourself a pep talk, allowing yourself to cry, or simply checking a map or your GPS (global positioning satellite) for directions. If you are near a restaurant, and you feel groggy, by all means, buy a cup of coffee or caffeinated soda to boost your mental alertness.

I also recommend that you drive your own car to events, even when you may be the guest of friends, since you will want to be free to either leave early or stay later at the event-- depending on your mood during that day or evening. It's best to have your own car and exercise your own power to do what is best for you.

IF per chance, you should feel uncomfortable driving home in your own car, you could choose to ride with whoever invited you and make arrangements to pick up your car the next day. Yet it would be a shame if you were having a great time and wished to stay a bit later at a party or event than the friends you rode with, yet you didn't have your own car to exercise that choice.

Alternatively, should you become uncomfortable at an event, and wish to leave earlier than your friends, you have your own car, and therefore your own power to do what is best for you.

Summary Takeaway:

Widows often don't know how they may feel at an event until they arrive and settle into the evening; so regardless of your mood, it's best to drive your own car. Then you can choose whether to leave early or stay late.

Chapter 32
Health Benefits of Socializing

I well realize that a widow is often invited to join a couple for dinner or a social outing only once. The apparent threat to couples' relationships and the awkward feeling of having a third person joining a couple apparently negates that second invitation.

Knowing that this is more true than false, there is no payoff in interpreting this as a personal affront or a sign that you are not good social company. It just is. Sadly, it happens.

IF you know of another widow, it may take some pressure off you and your widow friend to arrange social get-togethers with other singles or couples, so that the conversation and overall experience is easier.

Long after the covered dishes are frozen, thawed and eventually eaten or thrown out, widows need dinner invitations. If they are forthcoming, super. If they are not, please pick up the telephone and schedule a coffee, a meal, dessert and/or drinks, because it's a good bet that well-meaning folks may have said "let's have lunch" and just never followed up with a specific invitation, not wanting to intrude.

So, take your power and your calendar, and phone some of those very friends to put a date on the calendar--you'll both be glad you did. It's strange, yet true, that something as basic as having a couple of dates with friends on your calendar can boost your self-esteem and give you something to look forward to.

Additionally, attending a social event in a different or neighboring town may be less stressful than staying close to home. You may meet new people who share either a hobby or interest, or are also widowed.

Often women gather for dinner and a movie, or participate in a book club where you can get your mind and attention onto a good book or movie, and then look forward to a great discussion with others in the club. In this way, the attention is on the book/movie, and not on you, and you can listen to the people's comments and often determine who you might enjoy connecting with for lunch or coffee on a different day.

Singles-only as well as groups for specific hobbies abound and can be located on the Internet through www.MeetUp.com and myriad other sites. The lists grow each day. Or you might ask your local pastor, rabbi or priest and/or funeral director for listings. While any number of these people MAY have given or handed you information at the time of the funeral, it is quite likely you don't know where it is by the time you are ready to read it.

Group activities may include, yet are not limited to hiking, bird-watching, painting or drawing, scuba diving, travel, scrapbooking, singing, knitting, story-telling, crafts, tennis or handball, creative writing, kayaking, synchronized swimming, and the like. On your Internet browser, type in whatever sort of group you're interested in, and then choose the one that appeals to you.

Retreat centers offer excellent programs or simply hospitality space that you can utilize on a weekend or during the week. I served on the Board of Directors of Kirkridge Retreat Center www.Kirkridge.org and highly recommend their center, which offers breathtaking vistas and heart-healthy food, all on a modest budget. It is perched high in the mountains on the Appalachian Trail in Bangor, PA. Other women-friendly retreat centers include:

> www.Kripalu.org
> www.eOmega.org
> www.CanyonRanch.com

Again, search the Internet for a retreat center close to you, or hop a plane to one that appeals to your particular yearning(s).

Finally, widows need good friends--either ones they've known all along, or new ones that emerge during the grieving process. Widows do not need *certain* new friends who appear in time to cash in on media buzz, for example if the death has been determined wrongful. If you find yourself unable to ward off such persons, elicit the help of an old friend.

Right now you need to conserve all of your energy for yourself. The intent of people's friendships with you needs to center on their befriending you for your good, not for any anyone else's self-aggrandizement or to assuage anyone else's curiosities.

Summary Takeaway:

Arranging dates with friends for coffee or dinner is an essential step in our healing, as is seeking out new kindred spirits through book or movie clubs, perhaps in a neighboring town.

Chapter 33
Permission to Laugh

Laughing is vital to our health, especially before retiring to bed at night. Getting back in touch with your sense of humor is extraordinarily healthy because it releases serotonin, the happiness chemical, into the blood stream.

I'm dating myself here, yet might I suggest watching a few DVD episodes of Lucille Ball, Carol Burnett, Tim Conway, Harvey Korman, Gilda Radner, Art Linkletter, The Golden Girls, Tina Fey, Lily Tomlin, Robin Williams, Jerry Seinfeld or Jackie Mason?

According to www.WebMD.com and other sources, scientists across the globe have reported that laughter improves blood flow, enhances immune system response, and reduces blood sugar levels, as well as aids relaxation and sleep, all without the serious side-effects of drugs.

Maciej Buchowski, a Vanderbilt University scholar, even attests that 10-15 minutes of laughter burned 50 calories. Now, we're talking, gals!

Recent studies show that for ultimate health we should enjoy 12 laughs each and every day. And no, these can't be *carried over* from one day to the next like the cell phone plans of old. Enjoy them EACH and every day.

Summary Takeaway:

Not only does laughter evoke good feelings, it also releases serotonin into our blood, enhancing our psychological health and serving as a great natural sleep aid!

Chapter 34
I Am Still Pretty Cute!

I understand that many a widow's feeling of attractiveness dies with her husband. In other words, in the space of a single moment a *wife* becomes a *widow*. As a widow, you may feel bereft of your role as a wife, an attractive woman, or a sexy woman.

And without someone of primary importance to appreciate and comment on your beauty, you may well need encouragement to apply make-up, splash on perfume and dress in a stylish outfit--complete with your favorite shoes and designer bag.

Maybe you will choose to simply get comfortable with yourself looking attractive and sexy in the privacy of your home, or with your best friend invited over to share coffee or a cocktail. Then, next time you can progress to going to an event with a friend, or group of friends, and/or by yourself.

Or widows may choose to go to a social event in a different town, where they are not immediately known as "the widow who just lost her husband." The sense of anonymity can make it feel somehow safer to re-enter society, so to speak.

Whether or not you may repartner or remarry, you'll want to create a life that holds meaning for you. I realize that often the thought of remarriage or even meeting someone else romantically is an anathema to some widows, evoking very strong negative reactions, as if somehow even that **thought** could be an insult to your late husband and the marriage itself. Yet romance aside for now, it is indeed healthy to begin engaging in activities and hobbies that you find interesting, challenging or enjoyable.

It has been known to happen that in pursuing their interests, widows come in contact with people who share those same interests, which enable friendships to blossom, erasing some of the loneliness. And, you may even meet someone in those venues/meetings with whom you can socialize and/or even become romantic. Regardless, you'll have fun in the meantime.

Summary Takeaway:

Dress up in your most stylish outfit, don your favorite shoes and purse, apply the make-up and perfume and poof…you can't deny that you're one attractive babe!

Chapter 35
Less TV = More Brain Matter?

It is well documented that watching television causes you to feel like you have not had enough sleep, which ironically causes people to watch even more TV. If watched in excess, TV atrophies the mind in a way that many scientists believe can contribute to dementia.

If you have access to the Internet, type in the words, "How TV Atrophies the Mind" in your search engine, and you'll see hours' worth of fascinating, if not downright alarming, reading.

I recommend that you choose one or two of your favorite programs and set two alarms—the first to go off to **remind you to turn the TV on** for that particular program and the second to **remind you to turn the TV off** once that program is over. This will prevent you from having the TV on all the time.

I might suggest that you nickname your portable timers your "time coaches" or "meter maids"--whatever works for you--so that when they go off, you feel empowered and in control of your time and choices, not "bossed around" or in any sense, denied.

You have choices here, as in all areas of life. I congratulate you on DECIDING to exercise those choices. Perhaps the biggest choice (and victory) for all of us is taking control of how we invest our time.

Summary Takeaway:

While many widows admit having the TV on all the time provides much-desired background noise, it may not be that innocuous. It may actually contribute to dementia. Who dares to even risk such an outcome?

Chapter 36
Reading News/Listening to Music

Reading the news either from the newspaper or the Internet allows one to skip over topics that are too upsetting. Unlike watching the nightly news on TV, reading the parts of the news that appeal to you only takes a fraction of the time that is otherwise expended as reporters and advertisers blab on and on every evening. Many of us choose to read some GOOD news each day, right here at: www.dailygood.org.

Yet, if one must occasionally view the nightly news on TV rather than reading it, consider doing so at 6pm. This way your body and spirit have time to recover and get into a happier space prior to retiring each night. Watching the 11pm news and then attempting to fall into sleep shortly thereafter is not a great combination.

If you're like me, you have collections of compact discs filled with artist's gorgeous music spanning several genres. Why not dust them off and enjoy playing them now? Yes, I realize there are newer, more compact methods of storing music, yet regardless of the format in which it's delivered, music can provide either strong beats that we dance (or drum) to until we're exhausted, or soothing, comforting tones engendering quiet introspection and healing.

Alternatively, set your home or car radio to various memorized stations--classical, soft rock, pop, jazz, choral, etc., something for every mood. Let music be your background companion as it can either serve as a mood stabilizer or a mood enhancer--your choice.

Summary Takeaway:

Reading only the news you choose to know about, and listening to your collections of music playlists or CDs, limits the stress you allow in your life.

Chapter 37
Widowed, Yet Not Alone

There are currently millions of widows and widowers, and sadly, the number is growing with unprecedented speed. Additionally, according to the *New York Times* January 16, 2007 article entitled *51% of Women are Now Living without Spouses,* for the first time in American history, less than 50% of all women are now dependent on a male partner. While everyone's circumstances are certainly unique, and some of these very women have CHOSEN to live without a male partner, nonetheless, the presence of so many single women may serve as additional community for all of us.

Connecting with other people in similar circumstances (and specifically connecting with other women, as per Dr. Klein's UCLA study covered in Chapter 25) is comforting. And you will undoubtedly meet widows who have been widowed longer than you. This is valuable, but not because anyone else's pain is equal to or greater than yours. No one's situation is the same as yours, yet even a slight similarity will feel comforting, reassuring you you're not alone in feeling as you do; you're "normal."

Rather, meeting longer-term widows affords you the opportunity to see with your own eyes that other widows have also navigated the rough seas and emerged with new direction and meaning.

Yes, other widows have gained new confidence at taking back the drive-wheel of their lives. They've discovered new interests, hobbies and strengths that are carrying them through the voyage of their altered yet buoyant lives. It's one thing to know that this happens; it's quite another to witness it first-hand.

Summary Takeaway:

Widows abound: meet up and gain confidence in each other's courage, grit and successes.

Chapter 38
Widow's Myth Busters

I've heard these exact sentences from widows' mouths, so I wanted to share my answers, in the event you, too, may have the same misunderstandings as those in the examples that follow. I want to break these myths for you, so you don't waste time or opportunity by trusting any of them.

1. I should be expert in investing and financial planning, now that we have the Internet and 24-hour financial news, etc.

While the Internet and 24-hour news stations provide a plethora of information, they don't substitute for expertise and personalized planning.

Sorting through the information could take up all the allotted time for your finances, rather than your using that valuable time for decision-making on items you've discussed with your fee-only CFP®. While I know a little about medicine, for instance, I'd prefer to spend my free time on planning vacations and leisure activities, rather than treating myself medically.

The financial media also stokes a heightened importance to their message. Have you noticed how exercised the pundits get during market volatility? This is all staging and marketing, ladies; see it as such. It is entertainment, but surely not investment advice.

Rarely is any one single day's financial news important to your whole portfolio, and never should it evoke an investment action (buying or selling) in response! You will decide upon your investment discipline and map out the investments in a strategic meeting with your trusted CFP®. And then you will both monitor your results and progress towards achieving your goals, realizing that long-term goals will be solved with stock investments whose daily values will fluctuate widely.

2. I can invest inherited monies that my children received from their father (who died intestate) however I see fit.

When a married parent dies intestate (without a signed will), the surviving spouse may be required by her state's Surrogate Court to post a bond on the monies that the children inherit. (Laws of intestacy generally grant a certain fixed percentage of the decedent's estate to the surviving spouse and another fixed percentage to the children.) The surviving spouse may be required either to put said monies in a co-mingled account controlled by the Surrogate, or buy a bond for the money and invest it individually. The cost of the bond depends on the age of the child(ren) as well as the amount of money inherited, and easily could cost well into 5 figures. Seek the guidance and recommendations of a qualified estate settlement attorney.

3. I drafted my new will after my husband's death so my children will receive everything upon my death.

A will does NOT govern certain assets that pass by beneficiary designation, such as life insurance policies, annuities, IRAs, 401(k)s, 403(b)s, etc. Often the amount of these assets greatly supersedes the dollar amounts that your will governs, so check that all your beneficiary designations are correctly stated or better yet, file new beneficiary forms now just to make certain that everything is stated correctly.

4. My stock is down, but it's best to just hold it till it comes back.

It is seldom good practice to invest emotionally. Your CFP® may well advise selling a depressed mutual fund or stock, thereby locking in the capital loss. Capital losses offset capital gains dollar-for-dollar and then another $3,000 of additional losses can be deducted from your federal income tax return each year.

Uncle Sam shares in your capital losses as well as taxing your capital gains. Here's how it works. Let's say that due to sales in your portfolio during the year, you realized a $10,000 gain; i.e., the sale proceeds totaled $10,000 more than the price you originally paid--including all reinvested dividends. If that was the only activity in your investments that year, you would simply declare a $10,000 capital gain on your income taxes and pay the appropriate capital gains tax.

However, if you happened to have another investment that same year that had lost money since you invested in it, you may also choose to sell your losing investment.

For the sake of simplicity, let's say you're losing investment was down $10,000 from the price which you paid for it, so in selling that position, you would recognize a $10,000 capital loss. You may offset that loss against your similar dollar gain and, voila, you owe nothing! That's smart tax planning, and also smart investing.

IF after you offset all your gains with losses, you still happen to have additional losses, you would claim an additional $3,000 of losses each year. The net unused balance gets carried forward on your federal income tax return until it is used up. That $3,000 loss saves you income taxes. The exact amount will vary depending upon your other circumstances reported on your income tax return, yet suffice it to say, if you were in a 30% bracket, multiply your $3,000 loss times .30 and the approximate amount of taxes you saved is $900 on this $3,000 capital loss. I suspect you could figure out a use for $900, right?

So as to maintain exposure in that stock's sector, then, it is plausible that your CFP® would recommend buying another similar stock immediately. Since stocks within the same sector generally move together, you may reap the benefits of the sector recovery in your new stock while having pocketed the income tax savings resulting from recognizing the loss in the meantime. (If you are really fond of the exact stock that you sold, simply wait 30 days and buy it back, to avoid the 30-day wash sale rule. Be advised, however, that the price may fluctuate greatly in that 30-day period).

5. I won't need long-term care insurance because my children will care for me.

You will want to analyze whether long-term care insurance is right for you, but I dare say that many children would be ill-equipped to finance the ever escalating costs of health care for their parents.

You must qualify medically as well as be able to pay the premium for long-term care insurance. If your health is significantly impaired, you may not qualify to purchase individual long-term care insurance.

Inquire with any of the associations you belong to, or with your late husband's employer, to determine whether you could be accepted into any of their group medical insurance plans, especially if your health is impaired. A medical exam may not be necessary because groups underwrite a large pool of applicants and can afford to accept some higher risk individuals.

Absent carrying long-term care insurance, you could risk a partial or full spend-down of your estate, or you could obtain a reverse mortgage, should you require long-term care. Reverse mortgages are complex agreements that you would enter into only on trusted professional advice, as there are many choices that significantly affect your fees and flexibility.

6. I don't need life insurance.

Your fee-only CFP® will prepare an objective life insurance analysis to determine if coverage is necessary or not. I prefer to think of life insurance as *buying time* for the beneficiary. For example, if your annual salary is $100,000 and you wish to *buy* 6 years for those dependent upon you/your income to readjust without making huge financial or personal decisions, then I would be comfortable with your owning $600,000 of life insurance. If you would also want to eliminate a mortgage, or jump-start an education fund, for example, you would simply add those lump-sum figures to your earlier figure; buying an amount of insurance equal to that total. (Remember to subtract from the total that which you may already have via individual life insurance policies and/or group insurance benefits at work.)

7. The *tip* I just heard is really a *tip*.

In this information age, it is inconceivable that anyone would possess any information on a mutual fund or stock that high speed traders haven't already capitalized upon. It is my belief and that of myriad financial academics that the markets are priced 'efficiently,' which means that all the available information has already been factored into the price of each security.

Hence there is very little, if any, margin or arbitrage to be had--certainly not by the non-institutional investor, like you and me.

8. My children will act as adults in splitting up my estate upon my death.

Too many horror stories abound about the bickering and litigious activity of families after a death. Jimi Hendrix' estate was still being litigated 34+ years after his death. Michael Jackson's estate was litigated over 5 years; and look for Casey Kasem's estate to linger in the courts for a long while. Granted, these are famous people with lots of money, yet not-so-famous people also bicker.

Having your wishes written down legally never hurts those children who do act responsibly, but may be exceedingly valuable protection in the off-chance that even one child was to "act out."

9. Each of my heirs is money competent.

In a few families each member/child etc. is competent to manage money, but often the use of a trust and professional money management is the desired choice to better ensure an ongoing income stream and access to principal for one or more beneficiaries. Trusts also provide protection for the assets you've accumulated that can't be reached by your children's divorce or bankruptcy attorneys.

10. I'm confident my IRA trustee has current copies of my beneficiary designations.

Especially with the advent of stretch-out IRAs, many trustees are sorely lacking in their record keeping. Examples abound where the custodian claims not to have received updated forms.

It is imperative for you to locate a copy of your IRA beneficiary designation form(s). If you do not have these, ask your fee-only CFP® to complete and submit new beneficiary designation forms, mailing them via certified, return-receipt requested mail to the IRA plan custodian. If a trust will be the ultimate beneficiary, many custodians do not accept such a designation, so if you will be utilizing trusts as beneficiaries, ask the custodian if they will accept them. If not, change your custodian to one that will.

11. My general intelligence allows me to manage my own money effectively.

Many smart people delegate. Sometimes delegation is the smartest decision, since it's difficult for folks to separate their emotions from their money.

Rather than simply making arbitrary buy decisions and sell decisions, smart investors will first create a plan of action that incorporates their goals as well as their existing investments. They will then seek either to fill in the gaps or replace some assets with others more probable to achieve maximum risk-adjusted results, both in the short-term and the long-term.

Successful money management is a confluence of an art and a science. Disciplined portfolio construction incorporates effective diversification as well as systematic rebalancing of the portfolio back to the original mix of stocks and bonds. When was the last time you actually sold out of your winning mutual funds or stocks to purchase assets whose price was depressed to rebalance your portfolio and risk?

12. I should hold my stock options, or those of my late husband, right up until their expiry before I exercise them.

The timing of exercising stock options is dependent on a number of variables, and should be analyzed thoroughly rather than waiting until the last possible month or day before expiry.

13. I'm sure my investments are fine, as is.

Often families have a hodge-podge of investments that either someone has sold them or they bought years ago. When looked at as a whole portfolio, often there is duplication of assets. I've seen brokers fund an IRA with the exact same mutual funds that are held in an individual taxable account, for example. You can achieve much better diversification with attention to asset location rather than mirroring your holdings from one account to another.

Until you and your CFP® have mapped out your goals and run a Monte Carlo probability simulation, it would be nigh impossible to tell if your current portfolio will actually help you achieve your goals, even if your husband selected it. (Ouch, that may be painful).

14. I have 16 different mutual funds, so I am properly diversified.

Often investors purchase several mutual funds within the same fund family without realizing that the investment research permeates the entire fund family. This bias will likely tilt the portfolio either disproportionately towards growth or value, depending upon the company. The result may be that several of your mutual funds--all with different names mind you--will actually hold the very same stocks, causing significant stock overlap within your portfolio.

One may unknowingly have excess exposure in 4 or 5 particular large cap stocks, for example, which dilutes diversification and adds unnecessary standard deviation and risk.

15. I can't sell my low basis stock because I'll be clobbered with taxes.

Low basis stock can be dealt with in a number of ways. With current tax laws one would get the step-up in basis upon death, but that is hardly the optimum choice. Offsetting realized losses on the rest of one's portfolio would neutralize some of the gains.

Contributing a highly appreciated (read low basis) stock to a charitable remainder trust could result in a healthy income tax deduction and provide life income to you, the donor. Contributing a highly appreciated stock directly to a charity you adore would give you a handsome current income tax deduction, yet you will lose the entire value of that stock for income producing purposes in your portfolio.

If one resists the idea of any sale or an outright donated gift, however, a "put" may be in order to protect the downside price risk. If your low basis stock represents a highly concentrated position relative to your whole portfolio, then perhaps the use of a zero-cost collar--whereby you buy a "put" (an option to protect the downside) and sell a "call" (an option which limits your upside)--would be prudent until you have adequate losses in the remainder of your portfolio to offset the gains.

Whether or not you can achieve a zero cost collar--whether the money you receive from the "call option" will pay for the money you'd owe to buy the "put option"--would depend on both the particular dates and ensuing prices of both the put and the call. These are complications beyond the scope of this book, yet I want to give you a small taste of potential resources for myriad circumstances.

16. My attorney friend who closed my mortgage can handle my estate planning.

Legal professionals come in a variety of specialties, so please seek out a trust and estate lawyer for your estate planning documents. The nuances of estate planning are unique, and estate tax laws are ever changing, seemingly with each Congress.

The potential for financial loss is too great to entrust to anyone other than an estate planning specialist. If in doubt, seek a referral from your CFP® or Certified Public Accountant.

BONUS: I need to continue to grieve to honor the memory of my beloved.

I have every belief that your beloved realized, and realizes, how much you loved him, and indeed still possesses a certain "knowing" of how much you love him.

While this may sound woo-woo to you, consider that myriad widows speak of having experienced a terrific relief as a result of a "sign" from their husband, or a "feeling" that they connect to his energy. Invariably these signs convey a sense that your beloved is sending encouragement for you and for your future. If you are lucky enough for that to happen to you, I say, take all the comfort it was intended to convey.

Grieve, yes, and allow yourself to feel your feelings fully. Again, we can only heal when we allow ourselves to feel.

While each widow will somehow know the timing of when she can slowly proceed onward with creating her life, I want to share some research on our body's bio chemical makeup and flexibility around feeling and releasing feelings, including grief.

Jill Bolte Taylor is the Harvard neuro-anatomist who suffered a stroke and fully recovered some eight years later. She wrote, and I recommend your reading, her acclaimed book *My Stroke of Insight: A Brain Scientist's Personal Journey* New York: Viking, 2008.

Dr. Bolte Taylor tells us, "it takes 90 seconds for our bio chemistry to capture and then release our feelings within our bodies...so when you are sad, angry, or upset for any reason, allow yourself 90 seconds to fully feel those feelings, and then your body is bio chemically relieved of that feeling."

I also highly recommend Jill's TED talk at: www.ted.com/talks/jill_bolte_taylor_s_powerful_stroke_of_insight..

Summary Takeaway:

Question everything until you understand it. Now go forward, empowered and courageous women!

Chapter 39
Ongoing Monitoring

Obviously you have now selected a fee-only CERTIFIED FINANCIAL PLANNER™ and set up a comprehensive financial plan with strategies to achieve your goals, each with their own timeline. And while I don't want to tramp on anyone's toes, I feel these two terms--asset location and rebalancing--deserve some explaining as they are important to the success of any portfolio.

Be reminded that each investment plays a different role, much like golf clubs in a golf bag or spices in a kitchen cabinet. Investments are utilized to perform a certain function within your financial plan. Some investments will provide current income, some investments will provide future principal growth to keep pace with inflation, and some investments are designed to do a little of both.

Because investments and income taxes are inextricably connected, it's best to understand whether a particular investment will generate currently taxable earnings or not.

Asset Location

Yes, the **location** of assets matters. By that I mean, it's smartest to place assets that otherwise generate a lot of currently taxable income inside your IRA, for example. Tax-qualified is the industry name for any type of retirement savings plan with income tax advantages. A tax-qualified account will not be taxed currently. Rather, these earnings will accrue tax-deferred, under a tax umbrella as I like to think of it. So, with that as the back drop, can you see how putting bonds inside your IRA would save you paying current taxes?

These are nuances that your CFP® can handle for you, yet I want you to understand the possibilities for enhancing your return by the array of "finer" investing points, shall we say. This chapter covers two such examples of value-add; i.e., a confluence of financial planning's art and science all wrapped together. Your financial planner will serve your interests and give you money-saving ideas not only now, but also years and decades into the future.

Let's put some numbers on this verbiage. Say, for example, you have one regular investment account, and one IRA, and one Roth IRA, and you determine that the best mix of assets for you is 60% stocks and 40% bonds. It is **not** ideal to have each of these three accounts own 60% stocks and 40% bonds. Rather, the bulk of the bonds should sit within your IRA since all the earnings in an IRA grow tax-deferred until you withdraw them.

Since the Roth IRA offers you tax-FREE growth, your high growth assets, like stocks, would be best placed inside the Roth IRA, figuring that you would be getting a free tax ride on all the growth within that Roth IRA for your lifetime, presuming you held the assets 5 years. Your regular investment account would then contain some stocks and some bonds, to round out your overall portfolio.

Too many pundits speak only about the importance of asset allocation, and while I believe that asset allocation is ultimately going to dictate whether or not one meets their financial goals, I also believe in adding potential return to your portfolio by utilizing **Asset Location.**

So to review, since various assets carry different tax ramifications, in order to save paying excess income taxes along the way, why not save that money inside your accounts, and let it compound over the years? The intentional placement of various assets in either your taxable investment accounts or your tax-deferred accounts really does add value, some studies show it adding up to a quarter of one percent return annually.

Avoid the temptation then to compare one account's asset performance against that of another account's asset performance. Adopt the discipline to view your entire portfolio's performance--including all of your accounts. In my example that would entail looking at the gross performance on your taxable account(s), your IRA(s), and your Roth IRA(s), rather than any one singular account.

If properly constructed, when one asset is going down in value in one account, another asset will likely be going up in a different account. (This presumes of course, that your CFP® has paid attention to each asset class' correlation coefficients and invested as such.)

If the assets are **located** properly your Roth IRA performance will outshine your regular IRA account, due to each of their respective account holdings. I can well appreciate, however, that as an investor looking at all of your accounts, it's quite normal when you see one account performing quite differently than another, to want each account managed like that one which outperformed the others last quarter, or last year. Resist this temptation.

Admittedly I still have clients who upon receiving their quarterly performance statement, call asking for all their accounts to be invested like their Roth IRA, for example. No worries, I explain the concept of an entire portfolio, with different components, each of which solves a different risk and performance need, and all of which ultimately help you achieve your goals.

Granted, this process takes patience and discipline, yet this is why you will be best served to rely on a fee-only Certified Financial Planner™, with whom you will meet quarterly during the first several years, and then perhaps reduce the frequency to semiannually, or even annually, depending on your preference.

Rebalancing

A well-designed plan will not need to be tweaked often. Yet, when the value of the investments changes, as will happen over the months, you will understand why your advisor recommends selling off some of the gains in the better-performing asset classes in order to buy into the lesser-performing asset classes. Our mothers may have always told us, "buy low, and sell high" but in practice, that's a policy that's VERY hard to implement. Again, here's the value-add of a disciplined advisor, who doesn't get emotionally attached to any one asset.

I vividly remember telephoning a client with my recommendation that he sell some of his winners in order to invest those excess earnings into his lower priced assets. He balked and barked, very unhappy that I was proposing selling some of his "winners." Eventually he acquiesced to my recommendations, and within precisely two weeks the market had dropped in value so that because of that rebalancing move alone, he saved $60,000.

Granted, I've made my share of mistakes as well. Mistakes are going to happen whether you make them or your financial advisor makes them. Face that fact, and accept it. Judging yourself or your financial advisor is counterproductive at least, damning at worst. A quality CFP® will discuss mistakes and outline strategies to implement going forward.

In 36+ years as a financial planner and money manager, I've **never** encountered a financial mistake that couldn't be corrected and recovered from. Now put that in your perfectionist pipe and smoke it!

Summary Takeaway:

Congratulate yourself on completing a step-by-step journey to your financial empowerment. You Did It! Now, go enjoy what you're next going to check off of your very own bucket list.

Definitions of Useful Financial Terms

ACCREDITED ESTATE PLANNER – This AEP designation is awarded to select Attorneys, Chartered Life Underwriters, Certified Public Accountants, Certified Trust and Financial Advisors, Chartered Financial Consultants, and Certified Financial Planners™ who have a minimum of five years' experience engaged in estate planning and who fulfill rigorous requirements of education, experience, knowledge, professional reputation and character, as defined by the National Association of Estate Planners & Councils.

ACTIVE INVESTING – Investing in a stock or bond mutual fund or hedge fund where a manager or managers (or you, in the case of your purchase of an individual stock, bond, mutual fund or exchange traded fund) are buying and selling based upon research or gut feeling or trends in pursuit of adding value, or alpha.

Active managers charge higher fees than their passive manager counterparts, due to more trading as they buy and sell various stocks. Active investing contains more overhead costs to pay for research and analysts' salaries, etc.

The actual trading costs /commissions not only reduce your total return, they invite federal and state (if applicable) income tax on the extra transactions--insomuch as each trade would result in either a capital gain or a capital loss, which must be accounted for on your annual income tax return.

For example, if the index against which the active manager is competing returns 10%, the active manager must return on average, an extra 3% (or 13% total return) just to equal the net equivalent index return, due to fees. Warren Buffett and Peter Lynch, the two most revered stock pickers of our century, are both quoted as saying, "the best way to own common stocks is through index funds" and "most individual investors would be better off in an index mutual fund," respectively.

That said, my advice would be to resist the lure of the marketing sex appeal of seeing active manager's faces plastered on the cover of magazines luring us to buy their stock picks. Instead, save yourself money and choose passive investing for your investment portfolio.

ADJUSTED BASIS – the base price from which capital gains or losses upon the sale of an asset are calculated; generally the price paid for the investment, plus commissions paid, plus all reinvested dividends.

If any stock splits have occurred since the initial purchase, these also affect the adjusted basis. It is important to pay close attention to this calculation since it either lowers the capital gain (on which tax would be owed) or increases one's capital loss (on which a tax deduction is enjoyed).

ADJUSTED GROSS INCOME – An individual's (or couples') income before itemized deductions--these include but are not limited to, medical expenses, state & local income taxes, real estate taxes, allowable charitable contributions, etc. Various deductions are limited or eliminated, dependent upon one's adjusted gross income.

ANNUITY – An investment contract issued by an insurance company that provides for either systematic immediate or future payments. Payments may be for a fixed period of time or until the annuitant's death, or perhaps payable monthly for a period of at least 10, 15 or 20 years, typically referred to as a *period certain* payout.

Variable annuities offer choices of a stagnant guaranteed rate of fixed interest (for generally one year) and/or variable returns from a myriad of bond and stock sub-accounts. One can craft a diversified portfolio, investing in various types of sub-accounts, yet all earnings from a fixed or variable annuity are taxed at ORDINARY income tax brackets when withdrawn.

Generally ordinary income tax rates are much higher than those of capital gains, so the after-tax effect of annuity investing is critical to examine, as are the often exorbitant internal fees and expenses, which can easily total or exceed 3% a year.

Annuities are often "hard sold" especially to women, widows and seniors as a ploy to increase their meager interest rate yields on competing certificates of deposit. However, the long-term expenses of the annuities are onerous, due to the agents' commission often topping 10% of the initial amount invested. You do the math and then attempt to convince me that all annuity purchasers are suitable candidates. Choose **only no-load annuities** (no commission, recommended by fee-only CFPs®) IF you need to invest in annuities at all, which is extremely doubtful.

APPRECIATE – to increase in value. Generally we refer to one's principal investment (rather than any dividends or interest earned) as growing or increasing or appreciating in value.

BALANCE SHEET – An itemized statement listing all the total assets and all the total liabilities of an individual or business to illustrate its net worth at a given time.

BASIS (aka cost basis) – The cost--the price an investor pays, plus commission and reinvested dividends--of any investment. If one **inherits** a stock position, their basis is the price of the stock on the date of the decedent's death, or six months afterwards, if the estate is settled on what is called the alternate date; i.e., 6 months after the actual date of death. This is due to the step-up in a decedent's investment tax basis that occurs at their death to equal the market value, thus causing zero taxation upon immediate sale of such assets.

If one receives a **gift** of shares, their basis is the basis of whoever is giving them shares. In other words, if the grantor of the shares has a basis of $10 per share, regardless of what the shares are valued at upon the date of the gift, the giftee (recipient) will retain the grantor's $10. cost basis in this example.

BASIS POINT – One-hundredth of a percentage point (.01%). So for example, 100 basis points equal 1% and 50 basis points equal ½ of a percent. The phrase is usually used to describe either the return on an investment or the expenses of an investment.

BEAR MARKET – A stock market condition in which prices are falling--either sharp and quick or long and protracted--or expected to do so while the economy is in recession and unemployment is high. Generally a drop in stock prices of 20% or more is deemed a bear market.

BENEFICIARY – A person or entity named in a will, trust agreement, insurance policy, annuity contract, IRA, or other qualified retirement plan, that will receive financial benefits upon the death of the contract holder.

Assets requiring a beneficiary designation pass OUTSIDE one's will, so merely changing one's will and the beneficiaries within one's will does NOT govern life insurance, annuities, IRA accounts, Keoghs or other company-sponsored qualified retirement plans. These pass by virtue of the named beneficiary on the account application. Be SURE to file updated beneficiary designations to the requisite custodian (holder of those assets) especially after divorce, death of original beneficiary, or any significant family change.

BOND – A debt security issued by corporations, governments, or their agencies, in return for cash from lenders and investors. Interest-bearing bonds pay interest periodically. A bond holder is a creditor, not a shareholder.

BOND RATING – The estimate of the financial strength of a bond issuer, issued by Standard & Poor's, Moody's Investors Service and Fitch's Investors Service intended to inform investors of risks--principally default.

Bond ratings range from letters AAA to D, with B or lower ratings considered speculative; read potential loss of principal or interruption or suspension of interest. Bonds rated lower than BB are nicknamed "junk bonds," in that the issuing companies' balance sheet is either questionable, or they lack long-term track records of sales and/or earnings. They are more volatile in price and have to pay higher yields than higher-rated bonds to attract investors.

BULL MARKET – A market condition in which prices are rising, or expected to do so. A handy way to remember the difference between a bull market and a bear market is that a bull's horns generally curve upward; like an up/rising market, while a bear signifies a down market, akin to anyone in a bear of a mood...that's not good.

CAPITAL GAIN (or LOSS) – The difference between the sales price of a capital asset and the basis--price + commission + reinvested dividends--at which it was acquired. The capital gain or loss will be treated as long-term, if the security was held for a period exceeding 1 year and 1 day. Long-term capital gains receive a special (lower) federal income tax rate, currently 15%. Gains or losses on securities held for shorter durations are considered short-term, and are taxed at one's ordinary income tax bracket, which is generally higher than the capital gains rate.

CAPITAL GAINS TAX – Federal (and state, if applicable) income tax that is paid in the year in which a security's sale results in a gain. Gains on long-term capital assets--held longer than one year and one day--are taxed currently at rates up to 15%, where short duration capital gains are taxed at higher ordinary income rates.

CERTIFIED FINANCIAL PLANNER™ – An individual who has attained a bachelor's degree from an accredited U.S. college or university and who has completed an extensive series of training courses in specialty planning areas including, but not limited to: Employee Benefits, Investments, Income Tax, Insurance, Asset Protection, Retirement, Estate Planning, and Gift Tax and Transfers, and has passed a rigorous multi-hour CFP® Board Certification Exam, which tests one's knowledge of financial planning in real-world circumstances.

After passing the knowledge exam one must complete the equivalent of three years of full time employment in the financial planning industry, be approved by the CFP® Board, and agree to abide by the ongoing ethics and 30-hours of continuing education requirements every two years.

CERTIFICATE OF DEPOSIT – A certificate issued from a bank, stating the amount of money that has been lent them (from you as the investor) which they promise to return, along with a guaranteed amount of interest, pegged to a stated maturity date, usually between a few weeks and several years.

COMMODITY – A tradable item that can generally be further processed and sold; i.e., metals, wheat, coal, etc. Investors generally buy or sell through futures contracts.

COMPOUND INTEREST – Interest that is paid on both the principal and the accrued interest during the preceding period--computed annually, semiannually, quarterly, monthly or daily. The most frequent period of compound interest; i.e., daily, generates the largest return. So, when you attempt to read the plethora of rates on those small eye charts at the bank (I'm showing my age) pay attention to the APY--annual percentage yield. **The highest APY will occur with the interest compounded daily.**

CONSUMER PRICE INDEX (CPI) – The measure of changes in the cost of consumer goods, including housing, food, transportation, entertainment, medical care, etc. The US Department of Labor calculates the index each month from the cost of approximately 400 items in various urban areas across the United States. Some pensions and Social Security rely on the CPI to determine whether to issue increased payments to recipients to keep pace with the rising cost of living.

CORRECTION – a drop of more than 10% in the price of the stock market, during a bull (upward) market. Often a correction is temporary yet necessary in extended bull markets, so if you have extra money at those times, think of it as the stock market being on special sale and buy **more** then.

Remember, we want to buy LOW and sell HIGH, right? So while the masses are fearful and hand wringing, we WISE women will be grabbing up extra shares at a discount.

CORRELATION COEFFICIENT – a mathematical measurement of the degree to which one number will be affected by the change in another number.

Different securities whose prices move in the same direction will have a positive correlation coefficient and different securities whose prices move in opposite directions will have a negative correlation coefficient. Proper diversification requires selecting securities with low or negative correlation coefficients to each other.

CURRENT YIELD – The annual return on a bond is computed by dividing the annual coupon rate by the market price. The current yield equals the coupon rate when bonds are purchased at par; i.e., typically $1,000. Conversely the current yield exceeds the coupon rate for bonds purchased at a discount; i.e., typically less than $1,000.

CUSTODIAN – The company which holds certain types of taxable investments and tax-favored investments, such as IRAs, 401(k)s, 403(b)s, employer-provided qualified retirement plans, and the like. They issue reports/forms to the Federal Government alerting them when you transfer or withdraw funds.

DECEDENT – A person who has died.

DIVIDEND – The amount of a corporation's after-tax earnings that it pays to its shareholders who own common or preferred stock.

DOLLAR COST AVERAGING – DCA, as it's known in the financial world, is systematic purchases (or sales) of fixed-dollar (or fixed numbers of shares) at regular intervals. An investor buys more shares when the price is low and fewer shares when it rises, and the average price per share is often lower than that of purchasing a lump sum on any particular day. Automatic savings from your checking or savings account or via your 401(k), 403(b) or other retirement accounts, all utilize DCA, since the purchases happen routinely at a set interval.

DOW JONES INDEX – A leading index of U.S. stock market prices composed of 30 blue-chip, mostly industrial companies.

ESTATE – All assets owned by an individual at the time of their death, including but not limited to: financial investments, personal effects, collectibles, interest in businesses, real estate, titles to property, and evidences of ownership--such as owning one's own life insurance policy or a note receivable.

EXCHANGE TRADED FUND – A fund purchased and sold only through a broker. These trades thereby carry a commission. The ETF tracks a particular index, which trades like a stock insomuch as their price fluctuates second to second. Such funds are generally more tax-efficient than a traditional actively-traded mutual fund, yet opinion varies as to their tax and cost-efficiency compared to a passive index mutual fund.

Items to consider are that an ETF can be traded throughout the day as the price changes each moment, versus a passive index mutual fund, which is valued at each market's day's close. Yet the spread between the bid and the ask, coupled with the commission, as well as the fact that dividends are only reinvested quarterly, cause me to favor passive index mutual funds.

EXECUTOR – The person who, when named in a will carries out the decedent's wishes for the distribution of their assets. The executor (executrix when female) fulfills their duties under court supervision, and is entitled to charge the estate a fee for their services.

FDIC INSURANCE – The Federal Deposit Insurance Corporation insures each **owner** of an account at a participating institution (generally a bank) insurance on principal up to $250,000. If a couple owns a joint account worth $500,000 in the same bank, they each will be afforded $250,000 of coverage. If a husband owns an account worth $400,000 and has named his wife as an authorized withdrawer, the account will only be insured for $250,000, as his wife in this case is NOT an owner. You may obtain FDIC insurance over the $250,000 limit by establishing accounts in different ownership categories, including revocable (changeable) trust accounts, yet you should check with your institution first as to whether they are FDIC insured, and what the conditions are to obtain more than the up to $250,000 coverage.

If one owns a bank deposit account, and names her husband, mother, daughter and granddaughter equal beneficiaries, they may each be afforded extra FDIC coverage. Check the beneficiary's relationship to the account holder to determine whether additional coverage is afforded.

Finally, individual retirement accounts are generally afforded $250,000 in FDIC protection, per owner.

INDEX – A numerical measure of price movement in financial markets. Indexes measure the ups and downs of stock, bond, and some commodities markets. No one can invest directly in an index, per se; rather, one invests in either mutual funds of indexes or Exchange Traded Funds associated with various indexes, in order to hold the entirety of the index's basket of stocks or bonds or real estate.

INVESTMENT – An asset that is acquired for the purpose of producing income and/or capital gains.

LETTER OF TESTAMENTARY – a document issued by your local court signifying you are the legal executor for an estate.

LIQUIDITY – The ability of an investment to be easily converted into cash with little-to-no loss of capital and a minimum of delay, because of its high level of trading activity.

MARKET – A public place where buyers and sellers conduct transactions, usually in stocks, bonds, or commodities, either directly (individual stocks or individual bonds) or via intermediaries, like mutual funds or exchange traded funds, or limited partnerships, or hedge funds or structured products.

MONEY MARKET FUND – A mutual fund that invests only in short-term securities, such as banker's acceptances, commercial paper, repurchase agreements, and government bills. The net asset value per share is maintained at $1.00. Such funds are not federally insured, although the portfolio may consist of guaranteed securities or the fund may have private insurance protection.

MUNICIPAL BOND – A financial instrument that represents borrowing by state or local governments to pay for special projects such as highways or sewers. The interest that investors receive is generally exempt from some federal, state or city income taxes, although taxable municipal bonds do exist. Be sure to do your homework here rather than assuming any special tax treatment for your earnings.

MUTUAL FUND – Pools of money that are managed by an investment company and regulated by the Investment Company Act of 1940. They offer investors a variety of goals, depending on the fund and its investment charter and/or objective stated in the prospectus--that fat book written in legalese, required to accompany security sales pitches.

Some funds seek to generate income on a regular basis. Others seek to preserve an investor's money. Still others seek to invest in companies that are growing at a rapid pace.

Funds can impose a sales charge, or load, on investors when they buy or sell shares. Some funds also exact an annual marketing charge called a 12(b)1 fee, upwards of 1%. All these charges reduce your earnings; beware!

No-load funds impose no sales charge. Your CFP® can steer you to quality no-load, institutional mutual funds. Institutional mutual funds are less expensive than retail mutual funds, and are my clear preference.

Management expenses are disclosed in the prospectus and should be understood as a reduction in your earnings, so shop for lower expense mutual funds, which typically mean investing in index mutual funds, or institutional mutual funds, for example.

MUTUAL FUND FAMILY – A group of mutual funds set up by one investment company among which shareholders can easily switch or exchange shares (generally without charge) as their investment strategy or needs change. Most mutual fund families consist of several income and growth funds, precious metal funds, international, and specialty funds. You can obtain lower expenses if you invest amounts over certain "break points" within the mutual fund family. This practice is akin to quantity discounts at retail stores. So if you choose an excellent mutual fund family and invest in several of their funds, you will save expenses. Yet be sure to select a broad enough family to include both growth and value stock funds. You don't want to be invested in all growth stock funds or all value stock funds, simply to qualify for lower expenses. Be conscious of fees, yet do not allow the fee tail to wag the investment dog.

ORDINARY INCOME – The income derived from the regular operating activities of a company or individual's business. It is taxed at one's prevailing ordinary income tax rates because it does not qualify for special tax treatment, like reduced capital gains tax rates or any special averaging.

PASSIVE INVESTING – Investing in the entire market of stocks or bonds, believing that the markets are efficient; i.e., priced fairly without gross variances that may exist if someone knew something unique, or ahead of the rest of the market, in order to capitalize on that secret knowledge.

Passive investment expenses are razor thin by comparison to those of active management, since one owns the entire basket of stocks in whatever index they are invested. That is, if they wish to be invested in large US stocks, they may own all of the 500 stocks as represented by the Standard & Poor's 500 Index, for example. (An active management approach would NOT own all 500 stocks, but rather would select 100–200 of what that money manager/mutual fund manager deemed the best stocks of all the 500 stocks in the S&P 500 index).

Academic studies repeatedly show that 70–80% of the time, one would fare better owning an index fund of large capitalized stocks, than actively selecting individual names thereon. Peter Lynch, the brilliant former manager of The Magellan Fund, and Warren Buffett, CEO of Berkshire Hathaway (both renowned stock pickers) state that the average investor will do best in a passive investment, typically an index mutual fund.

PORTFOLIO – An investor's collection of investment holdings, including stocks, bonds, mutual funds, unit investment trusts, exchange traded funds, hedge funds, commodities, collectibles, real estate and almost any other type of asset. People may refer to their portfolio of investments versus their portfolio of real estate, or they may say, my portfolio to reference the totality of all their investments.

PRINCIPAL – The base amount invested plus or minus appreciation or depreciation. In other words, you invest X amount in an investment which is the market value at the moment you make that purchase. The price or market value will either appreciate (go up) or depreciate (go down) daily or perhaps every millisecond. Principal combined with any interest or dividend that your investment may generate, form the components of your investment's total return.

PROSPECTUS – A written legal document, required by the Securities Act of 1933, setting forth the complete history and current status of a security or fund. It must be made available whenever an offer to sell is made to the public. This is a huge amount of boiler plate legalese. Yet some very important information about the objective(s) of the fund, it risks and its expenses are easily identifiable, usually printed on the first few pages.

RETURN – The percentage change in the principal value of an investment over an evaluation period, including any distributions made from the portfolio during that period.

RISK – The measurable likelihood of loss or less-than-expected returns. It is often defined as the standard deviation of the return on total investment. While some consider this a four-letter word, risk IS the currency for return. So, realizing that, one can create a portfolio whereby the longer-term assets are invested in historically higher returning assets like stocks, whose price fluctuates widely in the short-term. Short-term bonds, whose price fluctuates far less, would be appropriate choices for one's shorter-term goals. For instance, if your retirement is over seven years away, you'll likely invest those monies in stocks; if a college education or a new boat goal is three years out, money markets, CDs or short-term bonds (whose price doesn't fluctuate as much in the short-term) would be suitable investment choices so you stand a better chance of having the exact amount on hand when you need it.

Purchasing power risk is that of sending hard earned money ahead in an under-performing investment that will not provide the return necessary to buy goods and services--a car, a house, or medical care--in the future because their prices increase due to **inflation**.

Investing is a bit like cooking; it is judicious to use the proper ingredient(s) for your specific recipe rather than just continuing to add salt because it's handy and you know how that tastes. Not every baked good stays in the oven for an hour, for example; some need more time than that. To follow that analogy, stocks need more time to grow than do bonds. That's why we WISE women investors will partner with our CFP® to match the timing of our goals with the most appropriate (or suitable, in financial vernacular) investments so that enough money will be available in our future, to buy the goods and services that we need or want.

SECURITY – The paper right that proves ownership of trade-able assets such as stocks, bonds, and other investments. These days, however, most people who invest in individual stocks or bonds "custody" or park the certificates with a financial institution. That parking ensures their safety and liquidity, which means the stock can be traded easily or turned into cash quickly, without having to 1) locate the security/certificate, and 2) sign an accompanying stock power (or the back of the security itself) in order to sell.

SIMPLE INTEREST – Interest that is paid on the initial investment alone and is calculated as a simple (not compound) percentage of the original principal amount.

STOCK – An ownership position (equity) in a corporation, issued in shares. The price of a stock will change potentially every millisecond, depending on the amount of buyers and sellers on any given day. While the value of some stocks gyrates wildly, typically one would invest monies earmarked for a long-term goal, such as 7+ years, in stocks or stock mutual funds.

STOCK SPLITS – These occur when a company decides to issue more shares to the public, sometimes following a run-up in the stock's price. The stock price itself is reduced by the amount of the split, yet because existing shareholders receive additional shares, the value of one's holdings does not change. If the company declares a 2:1 (two for one) split, and you owned 100 shares valued yesterday at $40 per share, today after the company's 2:1 stock split, you now own 200 shares, with each share valued at $20.00. In this example, both yesterday and today, your total value of that stock equals $4,000.

TREASURIES – Securities issued by the U.S. Department of the Treasury and backed by the US Federal Government against default. Treasury bills are obligations of the U.S. Treasury that have maturities of one year or less. They do not pay interest per se; they are instead sold at a discount to their "par" (i.e., maturing value), thus creating a positive return, generally referred to as a yield to maturity.

Treasury notes are debt obligations of the U.S. Treasury that have maturities of more than 2 years but less than 10 years and pay interest every 6 months, called a coupon payment. Treasury bonds are debt obligations of the U.S. Treasury that have maturities of 10 years or more, and like T-notes also pay a coupon (or interest) every six months.

VOLATILITY – The extent of fluctuation in share price, interest rates, etc. The higher the volatility, the less certain an investor is of a specific return on any specific day; therefore, volatility is one measure of risk. The VIX is not a salve you rub on your chest when you have a cold. The VIX is an indicator of the perceived level of volatility in the S&P 500 (large stocks) market for the next 30-days. It averaged 19.04 from 1990-October 2008, escalating to 89.53 on October 24, 2008. VIX values lower than 20 are benign, yet greater than 30 generally predict great investor fear, resulting in price volatility.

The discipline we must employ is to allow our long-term investments to grow without looking at their price every day. Unless you watch the price of your house every day while you are still living in it and have no intention of selling it in the next 5 years, don't watch the price of your stocks every day, or even every month. It's an exercise in information overload, and it could tempt you to take inappropriate action, kinda like jerking the cake outta the oven before it's done. You know the result; a fallen cake, which no one wants to eat but the dog, poor Skippy!

ZERO COUPON BOND – A bond in which no periodic coupon/interest is paid over the life of the contract. Instead, the "zero," as it's called, is purchased at a deeply discounted price, and then both the principal and the interest are paid at the maturity date.

If your zero coupon bond is tax-free you won't owe income taxes annually on the accrued interest. If your zero coupon bond is issued by a corporation, however, you will have to pay annual income tax on accrued interest; i.e., interest you don't actually receive until maturity. Best then to locate any corporate zero coupon bonds in an IRA for this reason.

Website Directory

Here are website links within the book in alphabetical order by topic:

BENEFITS (Potential) Sources:

- ➤ www.military.com/benefits/survivor-benefits/the-survivor-benefit-plan-explained.html-pg. 69
- ➤ www.militaryonesource.mil/12038/Project%20Documents/MilitaryHOMEFRONT/Casualty%20Assistance/Survivors%20Guide.pdf-pg. 69
- ➤ www.socialsecurity.gov-pgs. 69 & 114
- ➤ www.ssa.gov/survivorplan/survivorchartred.htm-pg.114
- ➤ www.va.gov-pg. 116
- ➤ www.aaa.com American Automobile Association-pg. 116
- ➤ www.aarp.org American Association of Retired Persons-pg. 116
- ➤ www.unclaimed.com–pg. 119
- ➤ www.unclaimedassets.com-pg. 119
- ➤ www.usgovinfo.about.com-Gov't assistance-pg. 119
- ➤ www.ehow.com Gov't assistance - pg. 120

CERTIFIED FINANCIAL PLANNER™ Sources:

- ➤ www.napfa.org-pg. 84
- ➤ www.garrettplanningnetwork.com–pg. 84

CHILDREN'S GRIEF HELP:

- ➤ www.Imaginenj.org-pg. 36
- ➤ www.drchristinahibbert.com-pg. 36
- ➤ www.TAPS.org-pg. 69

CREDIT SCORES & description of factors that matter:

- ➢ www.myfico.com-pg. 92
- ➢ www.AnnualCreditReport.com-FREE annual credit report-pg. 93

GRIEF COACH Source:

- ➢ www.griefrecoverymethod.com/outreach-program-pg. 35

HANGOUT (mostly women) for recipes/fashion/travel/inspiration, you name it there's a pin:

- ➢ www.Pinterest.com-pg. 165

HEALTH:

- ➢ www.foodforthought-healthstore.com Naturopath-pg. 171
- ➢ www.WebMD.com Medical research-pg. 190

IDENTITY THEFT:

- ➢ www.myfico.com-pg. 94
- ➢ www.lifelock.com-pg.94
- ➢ www.consumer.ftc.gov/-pg. 95

INCOME TAX-order past returns:

- ➢ www.irs.gov/uac/Newsroom/How-to-Get-a-Transcript-or-Copy-of-a-Prior-Year-Tax-Return-pg. 95
- ➢ www.irs.gov/Individuals/Get-Transcript-pg. 96

INSPIRATION:

- ➢ www.dailygood.org News that Inspires-pg. 196

➢ www.ted.com/talks/jill_bolte_taylor_s_powerfu
l_stroke_of_insight-pg. 212
➢ www.berniesiegelmd.com-pg. 4

INTERNET SEARCHES (type questions, get answers):

➢ www.Google.com-pg. 140
➢ www.YouTube.com-pg. 143

INTERNET PASSWORD MANAGER:

➢ www.LastPass.com-pg. 90

MEDITATION:

➢ www.chopra.com/community-pg. 182

MEET UPS-SIMILAR HOBBIES:

➢ www.MeetUp.com-pgs. 122 & 187

RETREAT-Widow or personal/program-centered:

➢ www.CampWidow.org-pg. 30
➢ www.SoaringSpirits.org-pg. 30
➢ www.TAPS.org-pg. 69
➢ www.Kirkridge.org-pg. 188
➢ www.Kripalu.org-pg. 188
➢ www.eOmega.org-pg. 188
➢ www.CanyonRanch.com-pg. 188

SEX TOYS:

➢ www.pureromance.com/shop/Adult-Sex-
Toys/For-Women-pg. 45

TRAVEL-SERVICE or RESEARCH TRIPS:

➢ www.globalvolunteers.org-pg. 168

> www.starfishvolunteers.com-pg. 168

TRAVEL-Singles and/or Cheap:

> www.lastminutetravel.com-pg. 180
> www.singlestravelintl.com-pg. 181
> www.worldtravelforsingles.com-pg.181
> www.solomatetravel.com-pg. 181

VOLUNTEERING-suggestions for how to give back or pay it forward:

> www.volunteermatch.org-pg. 168

WIDOW (& OTHER) BLOGS/FB PGS: Pgs. 152-153

> www.soaringspirits.org/resources/blog-roll
> www.freshwidow.blogspot.com/p/blogroll.html
> www.abigailcarter.com
> www.widowswearstilettos.com
> www.facebook.com/freshwidow
> www.facebook.com/LivingWithLossOneDayAtATime
> www.facebook.com/modernwidowsclub?fref=pb&hc_location=profile_browser
> www.facebook.com/2damnyoung?fref=pb&hc_location=profile_browser
> www.facebook.com/grieftheunspoken?fref=pb&hc_location=profile_browser
> www.facebook.com/TheWidowsJourney?fref=pb&hc_location=profile_browser
> www.grief.com
> www.calebwilde.com
> www.theloombafoundation.org/

Conclusion

Congratulations on your courage and your progress! You have the power to set your compass, select your crew, and fuel your mind and body to navigate your ship through both stormy and calm waters.

I invite you to find and nurture your unique essence and the mission for your life (and perhaps those of your children). You will be energized by your own creativity, your husband's guidance--which may appear in the strangest of ways--and also by making the soundest possible financial decisions from this day forward. We Can Do It Women!™

NEXT STEP

If you found this book helpful and would like to learn more, please check out my informative and easy-to-follow eCourse:

How We Women Can Be Better Investors

Visit www.DebraLMorrison.com/eCourse and enter the code *Book* for your deeply discounted tuition rate.

 C3